GOD

THE ULTIMATE HUMANITARIAN

The Story of How God Keeps on Giving

ISBN-13: 978-0-9974187-2-9

Table of Contents

Introduction

How do people view God? As a stern judge? As their best friend? As a distant deity? As a tolerant grandfather? These are just a few of many possibilities.

In 2010 the book *America's Four Gods*[1] was published. After conducting extensive research, the authors summarized Americans' most widely held views of God. They are:

- The authoritative God: judgmental and engaged
- The benevolent God: loving, not stern
- The critical God: not intervening now but will judge people later
- The distant God: disengaged after setting the universe in motion

There is no question that different views of God abound. But hardly, if ever, is God described as a humanitarian. Dictionaries define a humanitarian as someone who has concern for, or helps to improve, the

---

[1] Paul Froese and Christopher Bader, *America's Four Gods* (New York: Oxford University Press, 2010).

welfare and happiness of people even to the point of saving their lives. From beginning to end that is how the Bible describes the eternal God! Even though he is vastly superior to us, he tirelessly works for humanity from the moment of creation to the world's last day. Most importantly, he perfectly planned and executed the greatest humanitarian rescue mission of all time in the person of Jesus Christ. God is the ultimate humanitarian.

Far too often when we read the Bible we focus on what *God tells us to do*. There certainly is a place for that. But what is truly exciting is seeing what *God has done for us*. When we focus on his actions for us, we can remain assured of his acceptance even while being appalled by our sinfulness. By resting our hopes on Jesus' saving acts, we receive tremendous confidence and peace.

But not only does his love comfort us, it also energizes us. "We love *because he first loved us*" (1 John 4:19, my emphasis). His love is the only thing robust enough to motivate us to continue to love others no matter what. The more we comprehend God's stupendous love for us, the better we will reflect his love in our relationships.

In the following pages, I will be walking through the Bible from the viewpoint of God as a humanitarian. I pray that you will find this journey as exhilarating as I have.

Chapter One: A Humanitarian from the Beginning

Imagine being Adam and Eve at creation. What a blessing that God had singled them out for special attention. He created everything else in the universe simply by speaking. "Let it be" and everything instantaneously and perfectly came into existence – from the smallest atoms to the largest stars. But that's not how he created mankind. Instead of speaking, he figuratively got his hands dirty creating Adam. "Then the LORD God formed a man from the dust of the ground and breathed into his nostrils the breath of life, and the man became a living being" (Genesis 2:7).

God emphasized how extraordinary humanity was by creating Eve separately and uniquely. "So the LORD God caused the man to fall into a deep sleep; and while he was sleeping, he took one of the man's ribs and then closed up the place with flesh. Then the LORD God made a woman from the rib he had taken out of the man, and he brought her to the man" (Genesis 2:21-22). By deviating from his pattern of creating by simply speaking, God was demonstrating to Adam and Eve that they were special.

The human body reflects this. The greatest super-computers can't begin to duplicate the complex operations of the human brain. Artificial limbs, although wonderful, aren't nearly as good as the real thing. After spending millions of dollars and many years of effort, we still can't replicate the nervous system which allows us to tightly grip a hammer while alerting us to even the slightest cut on our fingers. Such examples are endless. This singular gift of the human body alone would qualify God as the ultimate humanitarian. No one has given mankind a better gift.

God, however, gave so much more! He created Adam and Eve in his own image. "So God created mankind in his own image, in the image of God he created them; male and female he created them" (Genesis 1:27). This was not a physical image but a spiritual one reflecting God's righteousness and holiness (Ephesians 4:24[2] and Colossians 3:10[3]). Mankind was the perfect crown of God's perfect creation. Adam and Eve were God's brilliant masterpieces.

God was just beginning. He continued by making Adam and Eve masters of his perfect creation. "God blessed them and said to them, 'Be fruitful and increase in number; fill the earth and subdue it. Rule over the fish in the sea and the birds in the sky and over every living creature that moves on the ground.' Then God said, 'I give you every seed-bearing plant on the face of the whole

---

[2] Ephesians 4:24 and to put on the new self, created to be like God in true righteousness and holiness.

[3] Colossians 3:10 and have put on the new self, which is being renewed in knowledge in the image of its Creator.

earth and every tree that has fruit with seed in it. They will be yours for food'" (Genesis 1:28-29).

Again imagine being Adam and Eve. Everywhere they turned they saw delightful new wonders: plants and trees in awesome variety, animals of every shape and size, a staggering assortment of grains and fruits. Think of the joy they experienced the first time they bit into any of the wide variety of fruit God had created.

Even the stars were created to serve mankind. "And God said, 'Let there be lights in the vault of the sky to separate the day from the night, and let them serve as signs to mark sacred times, and days and years, and let them be lights in the vault of the sky to give light on the earth.' And it was so" (Genesis 1:14-15).

God didn't just provide for their creature comforts either. He also provided for them emotionally by instituting marriage. "Then the LORD God made a woman from the rib he had taken out of the man, and he brought her to the man. The man said, 'This is now bone of my bones and flesh of my flesh; she shall be called "woman," for she was taken out of man.' That is why a man leaves his father and mother and is united to his wife, and they become one flesh" (Genesis 2:22-24).

Reading Genesis chapters 1 and 2 from the perspective of God being a humanitarian is an eye-opening, jaw-dropping experience. It emphasizes how good God is. It shows us that God doesn't just say nice-sounding things; he acts, mightily and wonderfully, for the good of mankind. God, the ultimate humanitarian, gave Adam and Eve a perfect life in a perfect paradise.

There's still more! Besides giving Adam and Eve perfect bodies, a perfect world to live in and rule over, and a perfect marriage, God also gave them a perfect relationship with him. Genesis describes God as walking and talking with them. This is utterly amazing because God is both unique and superior. There is no Being like him. He is the Creator. All others are his creations. He alone existed before creation. He is in a class totally by himself. In light of this, by establishing a relationship with Adam and Eve, God performed a mind-boggling act of love.

We see a hint of God's uniqueness already in Genesis 1:26. "Then God said, 'Let us make mankind in our image.'" The combination of the plural "us" with the singular "God" catches us off-guard. (If there is an "us," then we would normally expect "Gods.") As God continued to reveal himself down through the centuries, the mystery of his unique Being isn't solved – it only deepens. Other Bible passages make clear the "us" refers to three distinct persons: Father, Son, and Holy Spirit. The Bible, however, also clearly states there is only one God (e.g. 1 Corinthians 8:4[4]), even though in different places it

---

[4] 1 Corinthians 8:4 So then, about eating food sacrificed to idols: We know that "An idol is nothing at all in the world" and that "There is no God but one."

describes each of those three persons individually as God. The biblical revelation is that there is only one God consisting of three distinct persons – each who is fully God. When it comes to God's nature 1 + 1 + 1 = 1.

Does this make your head swim? I hope it does! The only correct view of God is one that blows our minds. God is so different from us and so far beyond us that we can't even begin to comprehend him. One sure sign of an incorrect view of God is thinking you understand him!

I like the way my friend illustrates this. He talks about God being on a vertical plane while humanity is on a horizontal plane. The only things we can know about God are the things lying at the junction where the planes meet. This junction is God's revelation in nature and most fully in the Bible. Thus the vast majority of God's nature and actions, everything else along the vertical plane, are unknowable to us.

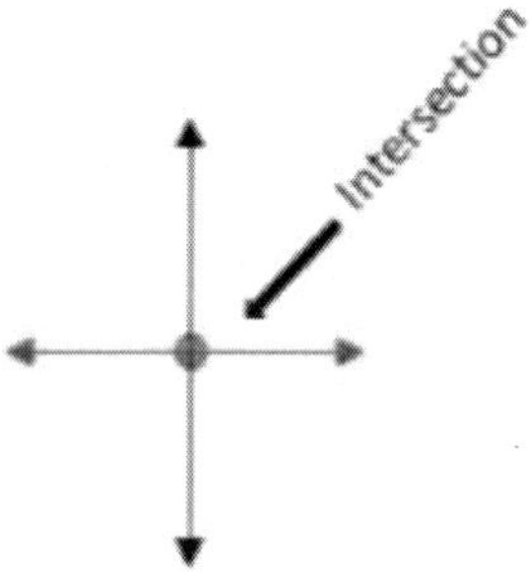

Countless people down through the centuries have been frustrated by God's incomprehensible nature. Two people who weren't frustrated were Adam and Eve.

Rather, they were in awe. They were amazed not only of who God was but also by what he had done for them. They were astonished at the wonderful gifts God had given them. Most importantly, they treasured God's eagerness to have a relationship with them.

When you stop and think about it, isn't it comforting to have a God who is vastly superior to us? A god we can understand; a god who is like us; or a god we can eventually become like – such a god is not impressive. But a God who is truly one of a kind; who created the universe effortlessly out of nothing; who made it so complex that still today we regularly discover new wonders – this is an impressive God.

At creation God revealed himself. We see his eternal nature in the fact that he alone existed before time began. We see his superiority in the fact that he is the Creator and everything else is his creation. We see his awesome power in his creation of the universe in six days. We see his stupendous wisdom in the intricacy and perfection of his creation. And we see he is a humanitarian. We see that he loves to shower gifts on the human race. God was a humanitarian from the beginning. And he was just beginning.

For Further Reflection

1. The Bible makes clear that the God of creation is the God consisting of three individual persons. It does this by attributing creation, in individual passages, to the

Father, Son, and Holy Spirit. The following are three of many such passages:

- 1 Corinthians 8:6 ascribes creation both to the Father and to the Son. "Yet for us there is but one God, the Father, from whom all things came and for whom we live; and there is but one Lord, Jesus Christ, through whom all things came and through whom we live."

- John 1:1-3, 14 speaks about the Son's work at creation: "In the beginning was the Word, and the Word was with God, and the Word was God. He was with God in the beginning. Through him all things were made; without him nothing was made that has been made. . . The Word became flesh and made his dwelling among us."

- Psalm 104:30 credits the Holy Spirit with creation. "When you send your Spirit, they are created."

2. The universe is so immense that we don't even know its outer limits. God, however, is greater than the universe. He fills the universe!

- Jeremiah 23:24: "'Who can hide in secret places so that I cannot see them?' declares the LORD. 'Do not I fill heaven and earth?' declares the LORD."

3. In Genesis 2 God is described as the "LORD God." "LORD" is the translation of the Hebrew word the Jewish people never spoke. It is God's proper name. In English it would be transliterated as *Jehovah* or *Jahweh*. "God," on the other hand, is the generic Hebrew word for God. In English it is *Elohim*. The title "LORD God" appears no less than 11 times in Genesis 2. It always refers to one Being. This then shows the error of saying Elohim is the Father and Jehovah or Jahweh is the Son. If that were the case then Genesis 2 would have to say, "The LORD and God." The incomprehensible God – Father, Son, and Holy Spirit – is the LORD God.

Chapter Two: A Humanitarian in the Face of Rebellion

Adam and Eve were literally living in paradise. Perfection, not problems, ruled the day. They enjoyed a frictionless relationship with each other and with God. The Lord had even given them an outlet to demonstrate their love to him; he commanded them not to eat from the tree of knowledge of good and evil (Genesis 2:17[5]). Martin Luther insightfully called the tree *man's first altar.* By obeying this command, Adam and Eve could express their worship and gratitude for all the great things God had given them.

Suddenly the story turns ominous. A serpent, who is more than a serpent, appears on the scene. The Bible reveals it was the devil speaking through the serpent (Revelation 12:9[6]). The devil was a perfect angel created by God who subsequently rebelled against God. 2 Peter 2:4 states: "For if God did not spare angels when they sinned, but sent them to hell, putting them in chains of darkness to be held for judgment." As a creature, the devil is vastly inferior to God.

---

[5] Genesis 2:17 "but you must not eat from the tree of the knowledge of good and evil, for when you eat from it you will certainly die."

[6] Revelation 12:9 The great dragon was hurled down – that ancient serpent called the devil, or Satan, who leads the whole world astray. He was hurled to the earth, and his angels with him.

The serpent casts doubt on what God had said. Eve is intrigued. "When the woman saw that the fruit of the tree was good for food and pleasing to the eye, and also desirable for gaining wisdom, she took some and ate it. She also gave some to her husband, who was with her, and he ate it" (Genesis 3:6). Tragically, she listened to the devil instead of God.

This impacted not only Adam and Eve, but the entire world. "Sin entered the world through one man, and death through sin, and in this way death came to all people, because all sinned" (Romans 5:12). Sin and death are two horrible words. We have gotten so accustomed to them that we struggle to see how hideous they truly are. From God's perspective the worst thing anybody can do is sin. And it doesn't matter what the sin is. Each and every sin is deserving of death. Without any qualifications the Bible states that "the wages of sin is death" (Romans 6:23).

No place is this better seen than with the first sin. From a human perspective eating a piece of fruit doesn't seem serious – at least not serious enough to bring sin and death to the entire human race!

That is why this story is so valuable. It reveals that the human perspective is wrong. It exposes the deadly nature of all sin. It underscores there are no harmless or minor sins. Sins are not simple mistakes. Every sin is an act of disrespect and rebellion against God. So much so that *even one sin makes people guilty of breaking all of God's commandments.*

"For whoever keeps the whole law and yet stumbles at just one point is guilty of breaking all of it" (James 2:10).

Guilty! This is exactly what the first sin made Adam and Eve. Not only them, but the entire human race. "One trespass resulted in *condemnation* for all people" (Romans 5:18, my emphasis).

Genesis 3 describes how sin's poison immediately took effect. Adam and Eve became spiritually dead, evidenced by the friction instantly appearing in their relationships. Instead of eagerly welcoming God, they fearfully hid from him. Instead of loving each other, they blamed each other.

They also became painfully aware of themselves. Before sin they were naked and unashamed. Immediately after they sinned they became ashamed of their nakedness. That God even asked a question about their nakedness (v. 11[7]) is instructive. It seems to imply that in their state of perfection they were not aware of themselves. This makes sense because perfection involves being totally focused on God. It was only after they sinned that they became self-aware and self-centered. Sin's poison had been released.

Imagine being God. He had made Adam and Eve the crown of his creation. He had showered them with one

---

[7] Genesis 3:11 And he said, "Who told you that you were naked? Have you eaten from the tree that I commanded you not to eat from?"

blessing after another. He had established a loving relationship with them. How do they respond? One gets the impression they hadn't been in paradise long before they tragically fell into sin. (We assume this because in their perfection they could and would have obeyed God's command to be fruitful and have children. Since no children were conceived in their perfect state we deduce they weren't in it very long.)

When temptation arrives in the voice of the serpent, they don't put up much of a fight. We don't hear of days and days of resistance before they finally cave. We don't see them fleeing temptation. And let's not just put the blame on Eve. The Bible places Adam with her (v. 6[8]) at the time of temptation. But we hear nothing from him! No objections; no warnings; no getting in the devil's face or standing up for God. Nothing.

Imagine being God and hearing Adam say, after all the blessings you had showered on him: "The woman *you put here with me* – she gave me some fruit from the tree, and I ate it" (Genesis 3:12, my emphasis). Talk about disrespect and rebellion. Talk about sin!

Imagine being God. Imagine the anger, the hurt, and the disappointment he could have rightfully had. So what

---

[8] Genesis 3:6 When the woman saw that the fruit of the tree was good for food and pleasing to the eye, and also desirable for gaining wisdom, she took some and ate it. She also gave some to her husband, who was with her, and he ate it.

does he do? *First take note of what he doesn't do.* He doesn't immediately destroy them. Neither does he wait for them to come to him with their heads hanging down. Instead he takes the initiative and goes to them! He gently draws a confession of sin out of them. He remains committed to them even when Adam dares to point the finger of blame at him!

Later in Genesis 3 we see God giving clothing to Adam and Eve. Even by driving them out of paradise, God was blessing them. If they would have remained, they would have eaten of the tree of life resulting in their living forever in their wretched, fallen state. In the face of terrible ingratitude and rebellion, God remained a humanitarian. He continued to act for the welfare of the human race.

No place is this better seen than in the middle of chapter 3. Yes, God speaks many words of judgment there. Twice the word "cursed" rings out. In neither case, however, does he curse Adam and Eve. He first curses Satan (v. 14[9]) and then the ground (v. 17[10]). Even taking that into consideration, however, his words to Adam and Eve are sobering. Because of sin they both would

---

[9] Genesis 3:14 So the LORD God said to the serpent, "Because you have done this, "Cursed are you above all livestock and all wild animals! You will crawl on your belly and you will eat dust all the days of your life."

[10] Genesis 3:17 To Adam he said, "Because you listened to your wife and ate fruit from the tree about which I commanded you, 'You must not eat from it,' "Cursed is the ground because of you; through painful toil you will eat food from it all the days of your life."

experience pain: she in childbirth, he in work. Because of sin they would experience friction with each other and with the created world. Because of sin their perfectly created bodies would turn to dust. Nothing good resulted ***from*** the fall.

At the fall, however, something good happened. We have already seen how God did not abandon mankind. Instead he sought them out and provided for them. But he gave them something much more valuable than clothing. *He gave them hope by giving them a promise of a Savior.* Speaking to Satan he says, "And I will put enmity between you and the woman, and between your offspring and hers; he will crush your head, and you will strike his heel" (Genesis 3:15). Note the singular "he" and "his" in the second part of the verse. Those singulars are highly significant. They show that God is not talking about the aversion many have to snakes, causing them to crush their heads. He is talking about *one offspring* who will crush, not the heads of snakes, but the head of "that ancient serpent called the devil, or Satan, who leads the whole world astray" (Revelation 12:9). God is referring to his own Son, Jesus Christ, defeating the devil for us.

Take a moment to marvel at this. Once again consider the setting. Adam and Eve had just ruined God's perfect creation. Animals turned into hunters and the hunted. Weeds suddenly appeared among the wheat. Fruit began to rot. Waves began to erode the shorelines. The entire world of nature was twisted, subjected to frustration and decay (Romans 8:20-21[11]). Through their disobedience Adam and Eve had wreaked havoc, not just on themselves, but on the entire world.

But God doesn't keep them hanging before giving them hope! Not even for a moment! He doesn't make them beg to be saved. He doesn't put them on probation seeing if they are worthy to be saved. Neither does he make his promise of a Savior conditional on their progression in goodness. There are no ifs, ands, or buts about it. A male offspring will crush Satan's head!

This is exactly what Jesus did. The inspired writer of the New Testament book of Hebrews, speaking of Jesus, wrote: "Since the children have flesh and blood, he too shared in their humanity so that by his death he might break the power of him who holds the power of death – that is, the devil – and free those who all their lives were held in slavery by their fear of death" (Hebrews 2:14-15).

In the Garden of Eden we see the beginning of a pattern which will continue until the end of time: God persistently showing love to the human race even though mankind persists in sinning against him. His is an

---

[11] Romans 8:20-21 For the creation was subjected to frustration, not by its own choice, but by the will of the one who subjected it, in hope that the creation itself will be liberated from its bondage to decay and brought into the freedom and glory of the children of God.

incredible, out of this world type of love. His is the love of the ultimate humanitarian.

For Further Reflection

Analyzing the devil's tactics with Eve is instructive. First note how he disguises himself. It is something both he and his human followers love to do. How they disguise themselves, however, catches many off guard. 2 Corinthians 11:14-15 states: "Satan himself masquerades as an angel of light. It is not surprising, then, if his servants also masquerade as servants of righteousness." In Matthew 7 Jesus warns about false prophets who come in sheep's clothing – who walk and talk like Christians, "but inwardly they are ferocious wolves" (Matthew 7:15).

One striking way that the devil and his followers masquerade as good is by using God's Word. In Genesis 3 the devil uses God's Word, questions it, and then twists it. We see him doing the same thing when he tempted Jesus (Matthew 4:6[12]). False teachers often do this as well. They take God's Word out of context; they use only parts of it; they define key terms differently; they twist it to mean something entirely different. One of the greatest dangers we face are teachers who look and sound so good, but who, in reality, are from the devil.

---

[12] Matthew 4:6 "If you are the Son of God," he said, "throw yourself down. For it is written: '"He will command his angels concerning you, and they will lift you up in their hands, so that you will not strike your foot against a stone.'"

Chapter Three: A Humanitarian to an Evil World

"This is the written account of Adam's family line. When God created mankind, he made them in the likeness of God. He created them male and female and blessed them. And he named them 'Mankind' when they were created. When Adam had lived 130 years, he had a son in his own likeness, in his own image; and he named him Seth" (Genesis 5:1-3).

At first reading these verses don't sound tragic. But they are. As they soberly report, Adam's descendants were born, not in God's holy image, but in Adam's sinful image. So much so that Adam's eldest son Cain killed Abel his brother in cold blood. So much so that Genesis 6 states man's wickedness had become so great that the Lord regretted he had made the human race. There, for the first time, we hear a chilling indictment of all mankind: "every inclination of the thoughts of the human heart was only evil all the time" (Genesis 6:5).

Genesis 6-8 describes how God sent a worldwide flood in response to human wickedness. It, however, did nothing to alter the condition of the human heart. After the flood, even though the world's population was 100% believers (Noah and his family), God repeated what he had said before the flood. "Never again will I curse the ground because of humans, even though every inclination of the human heart is evil from childhood" (Genesis 8:21). The flood, although it washed clean the world, did not cleanse the human heart. Centuries later Jesus said, "For out of the heart come evil thoughts – murder, adultery, sexual immorality, theft, false testimony, slander" (Matthew 15:19).

The ugly truth of the depravity of the human heart still holds true today. Therefore we must carefully consider God's diagnosis of our hearts – as painful as it might be.

As we study God's diagnosis, we see no exceptions. Every human is born with a depraved heart. It is not morally neutral. It is not inclined towards the good. *It is evil.* Not just weak and frail. Not just prone to harmless and minor faults. The divine verdict stands: the heart is evil.

It's not just partially evil either. The Lord said *every inclination* is evil. He didn't single out well-formed thoughts of mayhem and violence. He spoke of inclinations – passing whims and fleeting thoughts. Neither did he use the word "some." He said "*every* inclination is evil." *The human heart is pure evil.*

This is a very difficult truth to accept. As a result, many people try to water it down. But it remains the truth. It is not just terrorists and mass murderers who are evil. Because all are born in the sinful image of their parents, every single person is evil. "There is no one righteous, not even one; there is no one who understands; there is no one who seeks God. All have turned away, they have together become worthless; there is no one who does good, not even one" (Romans 3:10-12). The drumbeat of "no one…not even one…all" leaves no wiggle room.

Against the bleak background of this unvarnished truth, God's love for humanity shines brilliantly. Even the great flood benefited mankind, although it wiped out virtually the entire world's population. With the flood God hit the reset button, giving the human race still another chance. If God would have left the world to its own devices, it wouldn't have taken long for God's people and his truth to be wiped off the face of the earth.

Disengaging from his creation, however, is not God's nature. We saw that already in how he took the initiative with Adam and Eve after they sinned. We also see it here. He acts on behalf of mankind. He had every right to annihilate humanity. But he didn't. Even though mankind had caused him great pain, he saved Noah and his family. That is what humanitarians do.

Other examples of God's goodness abound in the story of the flood. God waited 120 years to unleash the raging waters of judgment. During those 120 years Noah sounded a warning about God's coming judgment. We know this because Peter calls Noah a "preacher of righteousness" (2 Peter 2:5[13]). God also saved at least two of every animal so we can still enjoy many of these wonderful creatures today.

We especially see his goodness in his dealings with Noah. He saved Noah and his family not because they were sinless. Shortly after the flood we read an ugly account of Noah's drunkenness and his son's disrespect. Noah wasn't sinless. But he was righteous (Genesis 6:9[14]). He was righteous through faith. "By faith Noah, when warned about things not yet seen, in holy fear built an ark to save his family. By his faith he condemned the world and became heir of the righteousness that is in keeping with faith" (Hebrews 11:7).

This introduces one of God's greatest humanitarian acts: his granting of Jesus' perfect righteousness through faith on individuals. A Google search of "righteousness" reveals it is used almost exclusively in religious contexts. Because of that, many people don't have a good grasp of its meaning. Righteousness describes something in line with, is "right" with, a set law. In the Bible, that is God's law. A person who is righteous is perfectly in line with all

---

[13] 2 Peter 2:5 if he did not spare the ancient world when he brought the flood on its ungodly people, but protected Noah, a preacher of righteousness, and seven others;

[14] Genesis 6:9 This is the account of Noah and his family. Noah was a righteous man, blameless among the people of his time, and he walked faithfully with God.

of God's law. In many passages, righteousness is equivalent to perfection.

As we have already seen, no one can achieve perfection themselves. "All have sinned and fall short of the glory of God" (Romans 3:23). Therefore God acted. His Son became human and lived a perfect life. Every one of Jesus' thoughts and actions was perfectly in line with God's law. Incredibly Jesus didn't do this for himself. He acted on behalf of all people. He lived, not so much as our example, but as our substitute. Examples show us what we have to do. Substitutes do it for us. Jesus lived to do for us what we couldn't do. "For just as through the disobedience of the one man the many were made sinners, so also through the obedience of the one man the many will be made righteous" (Romans 5:19). As if that wasn't enough, he then died to undo what we had done. "For Christ also suffered once for sins, the righteous for the unrighteous, to bring you to God" (1 Peter 3:18).

Here we come to the pinnacle of God's humanitarian action. It is one we will revisit often. Now, however, I want to emphasize the point made in Hebrews 11:7 (quoted above); namely, that people who lived before Christ were saved exactly like those living after him. They were saved by faith, by trusting in Christ's work for them – a fact the Bible consistently states.

This makes clear that Jesus didn't save us by setting an example and showing us what we are to do. There is no way Jesus could have served as an example for Noah because Noah died thousands of years before Jesus was even born. The only way Noah could be saved was if God credited him with Jesus' righteousness. This is exactly what happened. Noah and his family were saved, not because of anything they did, but solely on the basis of what Jesus would do for them.

In spite of God cleansing the world of unbelief, mankind's evilness quickly reared its ugly head again. Genesis reads like a tabloid with stories of intrigue, lust, rape, murder, and deceit. But through it also runs the golden thread of God's love. In the face of ongoing wickedness, God remained a humanitarian.

For Further Reflection

1. The Bible emphasizes in a number of different ways that everyone is born with a sin nature. As Job struggled under the burden of his great problems, he lamented, "Who can bring what is pure from the impure? No one!" (Job 14:4). King David went even further. As he came clean about his sin of adultery with Bathsheba he confessed: "Surely I was sinful at birth, sinful from the time my mother conceived me" (Psalm 51:5). Along with all the other things we inherited from our parents, we also inherited sin. In a way, we can say sin is part of our DNA. In spite of how startling this might sound, it does accentuate the fact we need help – we need a Savior!

2. Jesus said, before he comes again, the world would be in a similar situation as it was before the flood. "Just as it was in the days of Noah, so also will it be in the days of

the Son of Man. People were eating, drinking, marrying and being given in marriage up to the day Noah entered the ark. Then the flood came and destroyed them all" (Luke 17:26-27). Note that Jesus doesn't list any sinful activities per se. Rather he talks about everyday activities. This underscores the fact that even everyday activities can be evil when they are our primary focus. Being "world-focused" is a sin against the 1st Commandment.

Chapter Four: A Humanitarian by Making a Wonderful Covenant

Genesis 15 is one of the most fascinating chapters of Scripture. It opens with God giving a disheartened Abram a wonderful vision. (Abram is better known as Abraham, the name God gave him later in life.) Even though God had just granted him a great victory and had personally reassured him of his protection, Abram was discouraged.

The cause of his discouragement was not the fear of his enemies, but the lack of a son. This is understandable because years earlier God had given him a tremendous promise which relied on him having a son: "I will make you into a great nation, and I will bless you; I will make your name great, and you will be a blessing. I will bless those who bless you, and whoever curses you I will curse; and all peoples on earth will be blessed through you" (Genesis 12:2-3). Not only had God pledged to make him into a great nation, even more importantly, God had said all peoples on earth will be blessed through him. That was nothing less than a reference to Jesus, the Savior of the world![15]

---

[15] Peter applies this promise to Jesus in Acts 3:25. "And you are heirs of the prophets and of the covenant God made with your fathers. He said to Abraham, 'Through your offspring all peoples on earth will be blessed.'"

However the years went by and Abram remained childless. He wondered how God could fulfill this promise since both he and his wife were old.

So the Lord acted, not in anger because Abram doubted his word, but in compassion. The Lord "took him outside and said, 'Look up at the sky and count the stars – if indeed you can count them.' Then he said to him, 'So shall your offspring be'" (Genesis 15:5).

The next verse records Abram's response. "Abram *believed* the LORD, and he credited it to him as righteousness" (Genesis 15:6, my emphasis). This is the first mention of belief in the Bible. The New Testament writers recognized the significance of this verse by quoting it repeatedly. Paul's commentary is especially instructive. "What then shall we say that Abraham, our forefather according to the flesh, discovered in this matter? If, in fact, Abraham was justified by works, he had something to boast about – but not before God. What does Scripture say? 'Abraham believed God, and it was credited to him as righteousness.' Now to the one who works, wages are not credited as a gift but as an obligation. However, to the one who does not work but trusts God who justifies the ungodly, their faith is credited as righteousness" (Romans 4:1-5).

Abraham was righteous in the same way Noah was. Not by his own works but by trusting in God's promises to him. Trust is what faith is all about. Knowing something is true and trusting it are two completely different things. I might know the tightrope walker can carry me on his back as he walks the wire, but climbing on his back as he does so is something entirely different. Saving faith is abandoning all faith in my works and trusting only in Jesus' perfect work for me.

This introduction to faith makes Genesis 15 significant. What God does next makes it fascinating. He tells Abram to cut a goat and a ram in half and arrange the pieces in two rows. As darkness descends, he informs Abram that his descendants will be enslaved in Egypt for 400 years. But this isn't the end of the story. God continues and tells Abram that, after their time in Egypt, his descendants will return to Canaan and the land will become theirs. After the Lord shared this startling revelation we read: "When the sun had set and darkness had fallen, a smoking firepot with a blazing torch appeared and passed between the pieces" (Genesis 15:17).

What is that all about? To understand it, we need to know something about Abram's culture. This is how they enacted a covenant. A covenant is a formal contract between two parties. Today we make contracts official by having both parties sign it in the presence of a notary public. In Abram's day, they made covenants binding by doing what is described here: by cutting animals in half and having both parties walk between the pieces. In fact, the Hebrew expression for making a covenant is literally "cutting a covenant." This is the exact expression used in verse 18. "On that day the LORD made a covenant with Abram."

Abram, however, didn't walk through the pieces. Only the blazing torch which represented God did. That fact makes this account not only fascinating, but also tremendously comforting. In this striking way God impressed upon Abram that this covenant was *unilateral*. It did **not** depend on the faithfulness of both parties.

That is extraordinary. The vast majority of covenants are *bilateral*. Both parties must keep the terms in order for them to remain in force.

There were no terms for Abram to keep in the covenant God makes with him. God didn't say he would do this "if" Abram or his descendants would remain faithful. Neither did Abram make any promises. In fact, he doesn't say a word. It is all about God promising – God acting. He would give them the land. Period.

It's a good thing the covenant wasn't contingent on Abram's or his family's faithfulness. If it were, there would be no way they would have been worthy to inherit the land. The history of Abram's family mirrored that of mankind in general. Lies, deception, sexual immorality, murder – it's all there.

Permit me to pause for a moment to underscore the vital importance of seeing the significance of unilateral covenants. We are so accustomed to bilateral contracts that our default mode is to think every contract requires compliance by both parties. Not so. Unilateral covenants do not use the big word "if." Unilateral covenants, when made by God, are as good as done. There was no question whatsoever that Abram's descendants would possess the land.

Sometimes the covenants the Lord made were bilateral, contingent on human response. We will look at the most significant bilateral covenant in the next chapter. But the most important of all his covenants is unilateral. It is his "new covenant" that he introduces through the prophet Jeremiah. "'The days are coming,' declares the LORD, 'when I will make a new covenant with the people of Israel and with the people of Judah. It will not be like the covenant I made with their ancestors when I took them by the hand to lead them out of Egypt, because they broke my covenant, though I was a husband to them,' declares the LORD. 'This is the covenant I will make with the people of Israel after that time,' declares the LORD. 'I will put my law in their minds and write it on their hearts. I will be their God, and they will be my people. No longer will they teach their neighbor, or say to one another, "Know the LORD," because they will all know me, from the least of them to the greatest,' declares the LORD. 'For I will forgive their wickedness and will remember their sins no more'" (Jeremiah 31:31-34).

Note there are no "ifs." There are no conditions for mankind to meet. There are no requirements to be fulfilled. "I will forgive their wickedness and will remember their sins no more." Period.

The New Testament writers repeatedly speak of the new covenant. They make clear Jesus put it into effect through his sacrificial death for us. For example, talking about Jesus as our great priest, the book of Hebrews declares: "Day after day every priest stands and performs his religious duties; again and again he offers the same sacrifices, which can never take away sins. But when this priest had offered for all time one sacrifice for sins, he sat down at the right hand of God, and since that time he waits for his enemies to be made his footstool. *For by one sacrifice he has made perfect forever those who are being made holy.* The Holy Spirit also testifies to us about this. First he says: 'This is the covenant I will make with them after that time, says the Lord. I will put my laws in their hearts, and I will write them on their minds.' Then he adds: 'Their sins and lawless acts I will remember no more.' And where these have been forgiven, sacrifice for sin is no longer necessary" (Hebrews 10:11-18, my emphasis).

Talk about acting on behalf of mankind! Talk about being a humanitarian! God, acting unilaterally, punished his Son for our sins instead of punishing us. On the basis of Jesus' sacrificial death, God forgives mankind of their sins. *He forgives you of your sins.* Such love is unfathomable. Such is the love of the ultimate humanitarian.

For Further Reflection

1. The night before his crucifixion, Jesus connected the new covenant with his last supper. "In the same way, after the supper he took the cup, saying, 'This cup is the new covenant in my blood, which is poured out for you'" (Luke 22:20). This is one of the most profound statements ever spoken. And one of the most comforting. Jesus knows how we often struggle to be assured we are forgiven. Therefore in his supper he intimately, personally, and miraculously delivers his covenant, the forgiveness of sins. What he does for us in his supper is even more breathtaking than what he did for Abram. We will look at it in more depth in chapter 16.

2. James is another New Testament writer who quotes Genesis 15:6. He cites it to demonstrate the relationship between faith and works. By carefully reading James 2, we clearly see that God declared Abraham righteous *before* Abraham showed his faith by his works – especially by his willingness to sacrifice his son Isaac. The Bible consistently teaches that good works are a *result* of God declaring a person righteous because of their faith, not the *cause or reason* why God says a person is righteous. A believer's good works are the *fruits* of faith, (John 15:5[16]) not the *root*s from which salvation springs.

---

[16] John 15:5 "I am the vine; you are the branches. If you remain in me and I in you, you will bear much fruit; apart from me you can do nothing."

Chapter Five: A Humanitarian by Giving the Law

Just as the Lord had predicted to Abram, his descendants were enslaved in Egypt for 400 years. God then freed them by sending ten devastating plagues on Egypt. He also called Moses to lead them to the promised land. A couple of months into their journey, they arrived at Mt. Sinai.

There they experienced an awesome display of God's majesty. "On the morning of the third day there was thunder and lightning, with a thick cloud over the mountain, and a very loud trumpet blast. Everyone in the camp trembled. Then Moses led the people out of the camp to meet with God, and they stood at the foot of the mountain. Mount Sinai was covered with smoke, because the LORD descended on it in fire. The smoke billowed up from it like smoke from a furnace, and the whole mountain trembled violently. As the sound of the trumpet grew louder and louder, Moses spoke and the voice of God answered him" (Exodus 19:16-19).

This was just the prelude: God setting the stage. The main event was God himself speaking the Ten Commandments. Not only did he personally speak them, he also personally wrote them on two stone tablets. In these ways God highlighted their importance.

Why exactly are the Ten Commandments important? That is a most critical question. The correct answer can make the difference between life and death – eternal life and eternal death.

Before addressing that question, I need to digress to talk about the relationship between the law and the Ten Commandments. "Law" is a key biblical term with a variety of meanings. The original Hebrew word is Torah. Depending on the context, it can mean: 1) the entire Old Testament; 2) the first five books of the Old Testament; 3) the commands God gave on Mt. Sinai; 4) or God's commands in general. When the context is salvation, it usually means God's commands in general.

The Ten Commandments serve well as a summary of this broader sense. For example, God's prohibition against worrying is part of the law, even though the Ten Commandments don't specifically mention worry. In most cases when the discussion centers on salvation, the simple way to think of the law is to equate it with *God's commands.*

Let's return to the original question and rephrase it to make it broader. Why is *the law* so important? Stated another way: what were God's purposes for the law? Most people automatically think God gave commands as a way for people to win his favor by keeping them. After all, aren't laws enacted so they will be obeyed? It seems so logical.

But it is not biblical!

"Therefore no one will be declared righteous in God's sight by the works of the law; rather, through the law we become conscious of our sin" (Romans 3:20). This verse clearly states that no one wins God's approval, is "declared righteous," through obedience to his commandments. Instead his commands make us conscious of our disobedience, of our sins. God didn't give the law as a ladder enabling us to climb to heaven – each commandment being another rung on the ladder. Rather he gave the law as a mirror to show us our sins.

The law does this by issuing commands which are impossible for us to keep. This is a point most people don't see. Many think they keep the Ten Commandments. They don't understand that God doesn't command a superficial compliance. In Matthew chapters 5-7, Jesus brilliantly highlights the fallacy of such thinking. There he unpacks the essence of some of God's commands. He tells us God not only forbids actual murder but also hurtful words and even flashes of anger. Adultery includes lustful thoughts. On and on it goes. Jesus sums up his treatment of the law with the command to be perfect! A person cannot thoughtfully read those chapters without coming away with a deeper realization of the depth of their sinfulness.

Issuing impossible commands doesn't seem to be a humanitarian act. It looks more like God is cruelly toying with humanity. However that is only how it appears. At

Mt. Sinai God didn't break his pattern of working in mankind's best interests. He knew we had to see the seriousness of our sin problem before we would despair of our own goodness and cry out for help. Just like a doctor shows a patient X-rays to convince him he has cancer, so God uses the law as his X-ray to convince us that we are permeated with the cancer of sin. Then and only then are we eager to hear about his cure of a Savior.

The problem is that many people aren't inclined to see their sin. They are like people who cough occasionally, but otherwise feel fine. They first visit the doctor when the condition becomes advanced, only to hear the dreaded news that they have lung cancer. By then it's too late. They would have been so much better off with early detection.

God doesn't want people to avoid early detection of the seriousness of their sin. Therefore he did something about it. "The law was brought in *so that the trespass might increase*" (Romans 5:20, my emphasis). God used the law to bring to the surface the sin inherent in all of us.

We have all seen this principle in action. The little boy might not even notice the closed door until his mom tells him not to open it. Suddenly that is all he can think of. Before much time passes, he is opening it.

God wants to convince us that we are in terrible trouble before it is too late. Therefore he not only gave commandments to reveal our sinfulness, he also gave an abundance of commandments to make it abundantly clear how sinful we are. He did this even though the Son of God had to pay the price for every last sin.

This is how much God loves us. Even when it comes to making us aware of our sinful condition, he is the Great Physician. He is the ultimate humanitarian.

For Further Reflection

1. God's timing in giving the commandments is significant. He gave them *after* he had rescued Israel from Egypt. In other words, he didn't base his rescue on their keeping his commandments or on their worthiness. God emphasized this when Israel first arrived at Mt. Sinai. He began by pointing to what he had already done for them in Egypt. "You yourselves have seen what I did to Egypt, and how I carried you on eagles' wings and brought you to myself" (Exodus 19:4). Only then did he talk about their obedience. "Now if you obey me fully and keep my covenant, then out of all nations you will be my treasured possession." (Exodus 19:5*). Their obedience was to be in response to his goodness. It wasn't that he was good to them in response to their obedience.* The result of their obedience was not that he would save them, but that he would give them the additional blessing of being his treasured possession.

2. Unlike the unilateral covenant God made with Abram, the law was bilateral. It depended on the faithfulness of both parties. This is seen in the words quoted above: "Now if you obey me fully and keep my covenant." (The presence of the word "if" is always a good indication of a bilateral covenant.) Once we

understand that God gave the law to reveal sinfulness, it makes perfect sense to see it focused on human effort. In order to achieve its purpose of revealing sin, the covenant had to be bilateral.

3. It is enlightening to put Romans 3:20 and Galatians 3:24 side by side. This is especially true because Paul used the same Greek word in both passages. (Greek was the language the New Testament was originally written in.) In Romans 3:20 it is translated "declared righteous" and in Galatians 3:24 "justified." To make clear the comparison I have translated it "declared righteous" in both verses:

- Therefore no one will be declared righteous in God's sight by the works of the law (Romans 3:20).

- So the law was our guardian until Christ came that we might be declared righteous by faith (Galatians 3:24).

Putting those two verses side by side highlights the Bible's main message: God declares us righteous and welcomes people into his presence not because they have kept the commandments. Rather he does this because they trust that Jesus has done everything for them including keeping all the commandments.

Chapter Six: A Humanitarian at the Temple

Israel camped at Mt. Sinai for close to a year. During that time God provided them with detailed instructions concerning their worship. God designed it to contain numerous visuals of two fundamental spiritual truths: the seriousness of sin and the concept of substitutionary sacrifice. These visuals governed Israel's worship for the next 1,500 years.

On Mt. Sinai God gave Moses detailed blueprints for the tabernacle, the tent which was a predecessor of the temple. One of the most striking aspects of both the tabernacle and the temple was how restrictive access was. Only priests could enter them. This severely limited access because the Old Testament priesthood was restricted to 1) the male members of Aaron's family; and 2) those male members who had no physical defects. This excluded well over 99% of all Israelites! Except for a handful of priests, the Israelites could only proceed as far as the temple's courtyard. Imagine worshipping your entire life in the church's parking lot – never once entering the church. Imagine the message this would engrain in you about your lack of worthiness.

This is what the denial of access communicated loudly and clearly. God was telling them that *sin separates* mankind from him. He was emphasizing that he is holy and nothing unholy can survive in his presence. His holiness is like intense radiation which destroys any and all imperfections. Just as God gave the law to show mankind the *extent* of their sins, so he severely restricted access to the temple to teach Israel the *dire consequences* of sin. In this graphic way, he made clear that sin erects a wall between God and people.

He emphasized this in an even more striking way. Priests could only enter the first room of the temple. The inner room, variously called the Holy of Holies or the Most Holy Place, was one of the most highly restricted areas in all of history. Only one man, the high priest, could enter it. And he could only go in it one day a year! It was so severely restricted because it held the Ark of the Covenant, the symbol of God's presence. Only one man in a nation of millions, on only one day of the year, could even symbolically enter God's presence!

This vividly illustrated that sin is the great destroyer of mankind's relationship with God. God made this point so forcefully because sin not only destroys the relationship. It also blinds people to this fact. Many people assume that all is okay between God and themselves. They view sins as minor infractions, only deserving a slap on the wrist. They don't consider the possibility that each and every sin is a capital crime which merits death.

But a capital crime is exactly what each sin is. "The wages of sin is death" (Romans 6:23).

God's highlighting of sin's seriousness goes hand in hand with his giving of the law. His motive in both was to give mankind a figurative shake of the shoulders, an attempt to wake them up to the dire situation they were in.

When it came to the temple worship he instituted, God didn't stop with pointing out sin. His main goal was to teach them about his solution for sin.

He accomplished this brilliantly. The heart and core of temple worship was blood – blood sacrificed by one to take away the guilt of another. The main activity performed at the Old Testament temple was animal sacrifice. Day in and day out countless animals were butchered and sacrificed. At the temple dedication alone, Solomon sacrificed 22,000 cattle and 120,000 sheep and goats! (2 Chronicles 7:5[17]) The sights, sounds, and smells of the temple all screamed sacrifice.

Each sacrifice pointed ahead to Jesus, "the Lamb of God, who takes away the sin of the world" (John 1:29). The book of Hebrews further explains this. In reference to Old Testament sacrifices it states: "But those sacrifices are an annual reminder of sins. It is impossible for the blood of bulls and goats to take away sins" (Hebrews 10:3-4). It then continues with what Jesus, our

---

[17] 2 Chronicles 7:5 And King Solomon offered a sacrifice of twenty-two thousand head of cattle and a hundred and twenty thousand sheep and goats. So the king and all the people dedicated the temple of God.

high priest, did. "But when this priest had offered for all time one sacrifice for sins, he sat down at the right hand of God" (Hebrews 10:12). As our high priest, Jesus sacrificed himself for us.

That Jesus' death paid for all sin is something God gave dramatic proof of. At the moment of Jesus' death "the curtain of the temple was torn in two" (Luke 23:44). This curtain or veil had closed off the Holy of Holies for centuries. It had vividly symbolized that sin separates humanity from God. God now suddenly rips it wide open. He destroyed it because Jesus, by paying for the world's sin with his death, had reconciled God and mankind. "God was reconciling the world to himself in Christ, not counting people's sins against them" (2 Corinthians 5:19).

This fundamental principle – that reconciliation with God is achieved through the sacrifice of another – was reinforced every day at the temple. Before the animal was sacrificed, people would hold their hands over the animal's head and confess their sins. In this vivid way, they were symbolically transferring their sins to the animal. In light of that, imagine the effect this prophecy of the Messiah would have had on an Old Testament believer. "We all, like sheep, have gone astray, each of us has turned to our own way; and the LORD has laid on him [Jesus] the iniquity of us all" (Isaiah 53:6). This had to fill their hearts with joy as they realized God would save them, not by giving them an *example* to show them what they had to do, but rather by sending a *substitute* who would pay for their sins.

No place was this principle of salvation through a sacrifice of another more apparent than on the one day when the high priest entered the Holy of Holies. Before he entered, he had to offer various sacrifices to atone for himself, his family, and the entire nation. He would then take blood from each sacrifice, enter the Holy of Holies, and sprinkle it on the cover of the Ark of the Covenant. This graphically made the point that the only way people could approach God, and live to tell about it, was through blood.

The book of Hebrews mentions this, along with the tearing of the veil, to emphasize the tremendous access to God we now have through Jesus. "Therefore, brothers and sisters, since we have confidence to enter the Most Holy Place by the blood of Jesus, by a new and living way opened for us through the curtain, that is, his body, and since we have a great priest over the house of God, let us draw near to God with a sincere heart and with the full assurance that faith brings, having our hearts sprinkled to cleanse us from a guilty conscience and having our bodies washed with pure water" (Hebrews 10:19-22).

God designed the temple as his great classroom. Its structure stressed that sin separates mankind from God. Its sacrifices portrayed the principle of substitutionary sacrifice and pointed to Jesus who sacrificed himself for the world. The temple was not about people working for God. It was all about showing what God, the ultimate humanitarian, would do for humanity in Jesus Christ.

For Further Reflection

1. The day the high priest entered the Holy of Holies was called the Day of Atonement. (In Hebrew, the original language of the Old Testament, it is Yom Kippur.) There was something else the high priest did only on this day. He sent the scapegoat into the desert to die.

> But the goat chosen by lot as the scapegoat shall be presented alive before the LORD to be used for making atonement by sending it into the wilderness as a scapegoat. . . When Aaron has finished making atonement for the Most Holy Place, the tent of meeting and the altar, he shall bring forward the live goat. He is to lay both hands on the head of the live goat and confess over it all the wickedness and rebellion of the Israelites – all their sins – and put them on the goat's head. He shall send the goat away into the wilderness in the care of someone appointed for the task. The goat will carry on itself all their sins to a remote place; and the man shall release it in the wilderness (Leviticus 16:10, 20-22).

This was another way God pictured substitutionary sacrifice. Jesus was not only the Lamb of God, he was also the world's scapegoat.

2. With Jesus' death, the temple no longer had any reason for existence. Instead Paul asks believers: "Don't you know that you yourselves are God's temple and that God's Spirit dwells in your midst?" (1 Corinthians 3:16). What is so exhilarating about this statement is that the

Greek word for "temple" is the one used to describe the Holy of Holies! Because of Jesus' sacrifice, believers become the very thing that was off-limits in the Old Testament. They become the Holy of Holies, the place where God dwells.

3. Leviticus 22:21[18] required that animals sacrificed at the temple be without blemish. Peter refers to this: "For you know that it was not with perishable things such as silver or gold that you were redeemed from the empty way of life handed down to you from your ancestors, but with the precious blood of Christ, a lamb without blemish or defect" (1 Peter 1:18-19). To be an acceptable sacrifice Jesus had to be without blemish or defect. He had to be sinless.

---

[18] Leviticus 22:21 When anyone brings from the herd or flock a fellowship offering to the LORD to fulfill a special vow or as a freewill offering, it must be without defect or blemish to be acceptable.

Chapter Seven: A Humanitarian by Giving Mediators

The Old Testament contains examples of God's concern for mankind on almost every page. Tragically, however, many people don't see that. They think it portrays a harsh, even a vengeful, God. The Old Testament does speak many words of divine judgment. It also describes acts of divine judgment like the flood. Even God's judgments, however, are set against the background of his incredible patience. For example, he waited 120 years before unleashing the waters of the flood.

Words and acts of divine love are just as prominent in the Old Testament. I have highlighted a handful in the previous chapters. This chapter describes a final Old Testament example of God as a humanitarian. He graciously gave men who acted as mediators between the Israelites and himself.

Mediators were essential because of the great gulf sin had created between God and mankind. The Israelites didn't have the ability to bridge the gap, so the Lord bridged it for them. He created the three distinct positions (or offices) of prophet, priest, and king.

- *Prophets served as God's representatives to the people.* They were God's spokesmen; they brought divine revelations to the people.

- *Priests functioned as the people's representatives to God.* They brought the people's sacrifices to God. In addition, they interceded for the people in prayer.

- *Kings acted as God's shepherds of the people.* They provided for them and protected them.

It was an act of undeserved love for God to institute these offices. After all, he wasn't the one who had walked away from the relationship. Unexpectedly he continued to give Israel these mediators in spite of the nation's continued unfaithfulness. Israel, in large measure, did not follow God. It got so bad that God commanded one of his prophets, Hosea, to marry an adulterous woman as an illustration of God's relationship with Israel. God even commanded Hosea to buy his wife back (redeem her) when she was enslaved because of her prostitution. Not only was Hosea to redeem her. God also commanded him to continue to love her even though she had been repeatedly unfaithful to him. All this was a vivid demonstration of God's faithful love for unfaithful Israel.

Remarkably God persisted with this arrangement even when many of the mediators – the prophets, priests, and kings – weren't faithful to him. False prophets abounded. Wicked kings tyrannized the nation. Unscrupulous priests preyed on the innocent. So much so that God even sent the prophet Jeremiah to resist the false mediators: "Today I have made you a fortified city, an iron pillar and a bronze wall to stand against the whole land – against the kings of

Judah, its officials, its priests and the people of the land" (Jeremiah 1:18).

Thankfully there were also good mediators: kings who ruled unselfishly; priests who conscientiously represented the people to God; prophets who fearlessly proclaimed God's word. Through these men God richly blessed his people. His gift of these mediators is another example of his humanitarian efforts.

These Old Testament mediators, however, weren't his final solution. *Instead they pictured the final solution.* Just as all the sacrifices prefigured Jesus, so also these mediators. They were God's object lessons teaching Israel what the Messiah would do for them.

Jesus' connection with these mediators is evident already in his title "Messiah." Messiah is a Hebrew word meaning *The Anointed One.* In Greek, the language of the New Testament, it becomes the very familiar "Christ." By the title of "Messiah," or "Christ," Jesus was linked to these Old Testament mediators because all three types were installed into their roles by being anointed. Anointing signified that God had both appointed them to their office and equipped them with the Holy Spirit (1 Samuel 16:13[19]).

---

[19] 1 Samuel 16:13 So Samuel took the horn of oil and anointed him in the presence of his brothers, and from that day on the Spirit of the LORD came powerfully upon David.

Jesus was anointed with the Holy Spirit and power (Acts 10:38[20]). And he was anointed (appointed) not to just one of these positions but to all three. Furthermore, since he lives forever, he has no successors. ***Jesus is the ultimate and final prophet, priest, and king!***

He is the ultimate and final prophet. "In the past God spoke to our ancestors through the prophets at many times and in various ways, but in these last days he has spoken to us by his Son" (Hebrews 1:1-2). Note the contrast between the "past days" of the Old Testament and the "last days" of the New Testament. This contrast emphasizes that God has given his final revelation through his Son, thus signaling there is no more need for prophets. Jesus lives as the ultimate and final prophet.

He is the ultimate and final high priest. He offered the supreme sacrifice of his own life. "Unlike the other high priests, he does not need to offer sacrifices day after day, first for his own sins, and then for the sins of the people. He sacrificed for their sins once for all when he offered himself" (Hebrews 7:27). With his death Jesus, for all time, appeased God's wrath over sin. For all time he satisfied God's justice by completely paying sin's debt. And he did this for all people! "He is the atoning sacrifice for our sins, and not only for ours but also for the sins of the whole world" (1 John 2:2).

---

[20] Acts 10:38 how God anointed Jesus of Nazareth with the Holy Spirit and power, and how he went around doing good and healing all who were under the power of the devil, because God was with him.

His priestly work of sacrificing for us is completed. But his priestly work of interceding for us continues. "Therefore he is able to save completely those who come to God through him, because he always lives to intercede for them" (Hebrews 7:25). Jesus lives as the ultimate and final high priest.

He is the ultimate and final king. "And God placed all things under his feet and appointed him to be head over everything for the church, which is his body, the fullness of him who fills everything in every way" (Ephesians 1:22-23). Jesus rules "for the church." He directs events in such a way that they always benefit the people who trust in him. "And we know that in all things God works for the good of those who love him, who have been called according to his purpose" (Romans 8:28). Jesus lives as the ultimate and final king.

Pause for a moment to savor the comfort of having Jesus as your prophet, priest, and king. Since he is your living prophet, you don't have to look for other prophets. Since he is your living priest, you can be assured that all your sins have been completely forgiven – for God would never have allowed a false messiah to rise from the dead. Since he is your living king, you don't have to fret about sinful people being in control – because they aren't. King Jesus is the one who controls all things. As prophet, priest, and king, Jesus is the epitome of the ultimate humanitarian.

For Further Reflection

1. Another Old Testament priest who prefigured Jesus was Melchizedek. This is surprising since he appears so briefly (Genesis 14:18-20[21]). He blesses Abram and Abram gave him a tithe. Then we hear nothing else about him until Psalm 110 – a wonderful psalm about the coming Messiah. There we hear the Father telling the Son: "You are a priest forever, in the order of Melchizedek" (v. 4). The Old Testament doesn't mention Melchizedek again.

Thankfully the book of Hebrews explains his significance. It does this in great detail, dedicating close to three chapters (5-7). It describes how Melchizedek foreshadowed Christ. It makes the important point that Jesus' coming marked the end of the Aaronic priesthood. (The Aaronic priesthood was the one God established for Old Testament Israel. It is called Aaronic because every priest had to be a descendant of Aaron.) At Jesus' coming the Melchizedek priesthood replaced the Aaronic. But because Jesus lives forever, he is the only priest in it! "Now there have been many of those priests, since death prevented them from continuing in office; but because Jesus lives forever, he has a permanent priesthood" (Hebrews 7:23-24).

---

[21] Genesis 14:18-20 Then Melchizedek king of Salem brought out bread and wine. He was priest of God Most High, and he blessed Abram, saying, "Blessed be Abram by God Most High, Creator of heaven and earth. And praise be to God Most High, who delivered your enemies into your hand." Then Abram gave him a tenth of everything.

2. Another exciting passage is 1 Peter 2:9. Addressing believers it says: "But you are a chosen people, a royal priesthood." It doesn't say believers are in any "order" of priesthood. Rather, it emphasizes that every believer, regardless of their sex or age, are priests. This underscores that we no longer need any other mediator except Jesus. "For there is one God and one mediator between God and mankind, the man Christ Jesus" (1 Timothy 2:5). Every believer has direct access to God.

Chapter Eight: A Humanitarian by Becoming Man

"But when the set time had fully come, God sent his Son, born of a woman, born under the law, to redeem those under the law, that we might receive adoption to sonship" (Galatians 4:4-5). The time had finally arrived to which the whole Old Testament had been building. Hundreds of prophecies had pointed to Jesus and countless sacrifices had symbolized him. The supreme significance of Jesus' birth is even seen in how people worldwide and throughout history use it to divide the years between BC and AD.[22]

There are many ways to think about Christmas. One of my favorites is to view it as a deployment. This is what the above verse states. The Greek word used for "sent" literally means "send on a mission." God deployed his Son on a rescue mission. He came to "redeem those under the law."

The only way the Son of God could do this, however, was by taking our place. He couldn't rescue us by just teaching us what we needed to do. Because sin had brainwashed humanity, we needed more than a teacher. Neither could he save us by showing us what to do.

---

[22] BC stands for "Before Christ" while AD comes from the Latin and means "in the year of our Lord"

Because sin had incapacitated humanity, we needed more than an example. Nor could he help us by doing some of the work while we did the rest. Because sin had spiritually killed humanity, we needed more than a hand up. *We needed somebody to do it all for us. We needed a substitute* (Isaiah 53:5-6[23]).

To be our substitute, the Son of God had to become human. He had to be human to die. "Since the children have flesh and blood, he too shared in their humanity so that by his death he might break the power of him who holds the power of death – that is, the devil – and free those who all their lives were held in slavery by their fear of death" (Hebrews 2:14-15).

This is another one of those incomprehensible truths which are peppered throughout the Bible. There is no way the human mind can fathom how one person can be both fully God and fully human. Skeptics dismiss this and say the finite cannot contain the infinite. Scripture, however, says: "in Christ all the fullness of the Deity lives in bodily form" (Colossians 2:9).

God already emphasized at his birth that Jesus was both God and man. In connection with the angel's announcement of Jesus' birth to Joseph, Matthew's gospel

---

[23] Isaiah 53:5-6 But he was pierced for our transgressions, he was crushed for our iniquities; the punishment that brought us peace was on him, and by his wounds we are healed. We all, like sheep, have gone astray, each of us has turned to our own way; and the LORD has laid on him the iniquity of us all.

states: "All this took place to fulfill what the Lord had said through the prophet: 'The virgin will conceive and give birth to a son, and they will call him Immanuel' (which means 'God with us')" (Matthew 1:22-23). Jesus was God with us. He was the God-man.

In order to save us, he had to be both God and man. He had to be man to serve as mankind's substitute. He had to be God because only God could serve as a substitute *for all humanity*. "No one can redeem the life of another or give to God a ransom for them – the ransom for a life is costly, no payment is ever enough" (Psalm 49:7-8).

There's more. The Son of God did not only have to become *human,* he also had to become *humble.* Philippians 2:6-8 is one passage which teaches this. It's not the easiest section to understand but it's well worth the effort. A correct understanding is the key which unlocks numerous other passages.

It reads: "Who, being in very nature God, did not consider equality with God something to be used to his own advantage; rather, he made himself nothing by taking the very nature of a servant, being made in human likeness. And being found in appearance as a man, he humbled himself by becoming obedient to death – even death on a cross!"

The first thing of note is the contrast between the two natures attributed to Jesus. It begins by affirming his *very nature as God.* There never was a time when he wasn't God. From all eternity he has been God. It then says he made himself nothing and took on the *very nature of a servant.* The Greek word translated servant literally means slave. The one thing every slave has is a master. Even though Jesus was always God and master of all, he voluntarily took a slave nature and became the slave of a master.

His master was none other than his Father. This is fundamental to understanding Jesus' statements that he was subordinate to his Father – statements like "the Father is greater than I" (John 14:28). This makes perfect sense in light of Jesus taking upon himself the nature of a slave. Masters are greater than slaves. The Father was not greater than Jesus according to their essential natures. It's in the context of his mission of humbling himself that the Father is greater than the Son.

There are no analogies which do justice to what Jesus did. Hopefully the following illustration helps. Imagine a king, in order to learn what his citizens thought of him, disguised himself, mingled with the populace, and got into conversations about how the king governed. In such a scenario, it's easy to imagine the king talking about himself as his superior. So much so that any listener would scoff at the idea that the man talking was equal to the king.

As I said, no analogy does justice to what Jesus did. He didn't just come in the disguise of a slave; he took on the very nature of a slave. For his entire earthly life, he did his Father's bidding – a fact which surfaces more than once. For example, note the "slave" language of obedience in Philippians 2: "by becoming obedient to death." This brings to mind Jesus' prayer in Gethsemane. "My Father, if it is possible, may this cup be taken from me. Yet not as I will, but as you will" (Matthew 26:39).

Jesus' humbling of himself was an essential aspect of his rescuing us. "For you know the grace of our Lord Jesus Christ, that though he was rich, yet for your sake he became poor, so that you through his poverty might become rich" (2 Corinthians 8:9). It was through his poverty, his life as a slave, that we received the riches of eternal life.

The thought of the Son of God humbling himself staggers us. We struggle to wrap our minds around the fact that the King of the universe was born in much humbler circumstances than probably any of us were. But it wasn't just his birth. His entire life was humble. During his ministry Jesus said: "Foxes have dens and birds have nests, but the Son of Man has no place to lay his head" (Matthew 8:20). He, who for all eternity lived in tremendous heavenly glory, had an extremely low standard of living.

His sole purpose for living like this was to save us. His humble lifestyle wasn't forced on him. He chose it. "He made himself nothing." And he did that for people who, for the most part, didn't appreciate it. You can almost hear John's sadness as he reports: "He came to that which was his own, but his own did not receive him" (John 1:11).

View Christmas from God's perspective. Imagine being the Father deploying his Son on a mission which you know will involve his horrible death. Imagine the Son, the Master of all, becoming a humble slave – not just for a few days but for an entire life. Imagine doing this knowing full well the vast majority of people won't just be unappreciative; they will violently reject you. Imagine sending your Son to save terrorists – imagine yourself going to save terrorists – who will torture and kill you.

This is a pale comparison of what God did at Christmas. This is why God is the ultimate humanitarian.

For Further Reflection

1. An essential aspect of Christmas is Jesus being born of a virgin, something prophesied 700 years before. "Therefore the Lord himself will give you a sign: The virgin will conceive and give birth to a son, and will call him Immanuel" (Isaiah 7:14). In answer to Mary's question of how she could give birth, the angel Gabriel replied: "The Holy Spirit will come on you, and the power of the Most High will overshadow you. So the holy one to be born will be called the Son of God" (Luke 1:35). What Gabriel describes is far beyond human understanding. Some biblical scholars point to the original Greek word for "to be born" and note not only is it in the present tense but it also can mean *conceive*. For example, W. Arndt puts it this way: "the Holy Being that was now being conceived

would be called the Son of God."[24] Jesus' conception was not natural. It was supernatural.

2. Note that, in the above verse, Gabriel calls Jesus "the holy one." The Bible clearly says Jesus was without sin (Hebrews 4:15[25]). He never committed even one sin. Because he was miraculously conceived by the Holy Spirit, neither did he inherit a sin nature from Mary. This is another reason why Jesus' wonderful conception and birth are so significant.

---

[24] William F. Arndt, *Bible Commentary: St. Luke* (Concordia, 1956), p. 51.

[25] Hebrews 4:15 For we do not have a high priest who is unable to empathize with our weaknesses, but we have one who has been tempted in every way, just as we are – yet he did not sin.

Chapter Nine: A Humanitarian by Living for Us

Imagine having an obnoxious neighbor who constantly harasses you. It's so bad that you do whatever you can to avoid him. Then one day he gets into a car accident which leaves him paralyzed. You drop everything to take care of him night and day – even though he can't pay you a dime. You sacrifice greatly for him, but his attitude doesn't change. He still treats you rudely and doesn't give you even one word of appreciation.

Can you see yourself doing this? I confess I can't see myself in this picture. The best I can see is reluctantly offering to help him temporarily and then storming out at his first insult. Even doing that much, however, would be a stretch. There is no way I would remain in the face of ingratitude and harassment.

It's extremely difficult living day in and day out for somebody else – even for a loved one who is very appreciative. Care-giving requires a lot of commitment. It is difficult imagining anybody continuing to sacrifice for such an ungrateful man.

This scenario is a weak analogy of what Jesus did for us. I like to say Jesus sacrificed his life *twice* for us. He not only died for us; he also lived for us. With his death he washed away our sins and with his life he kept the law perfectly for us. Both are essential for our salvation. What makes this all the more amazing is that Jesus did this for people who were worse than the obnoxious neighbor. He did this for people whom he had wonderfully created but who had sinfully defied him every step of the way.

Over the years I have given a simple test to thousands of Christians to see if they understood that Jesus both lived and died for them. The vast majority have failed it. Here it is.

This first heart filled with plus signs symbolizes the perfection needed to enter heaven.

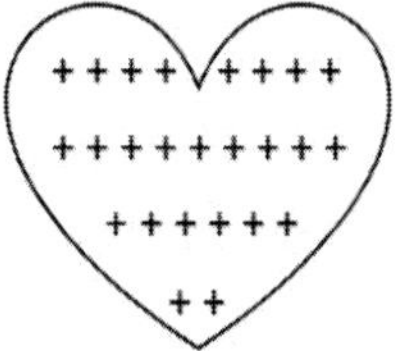

This second heart filled with minus signs symbolizes our hearts of sin.

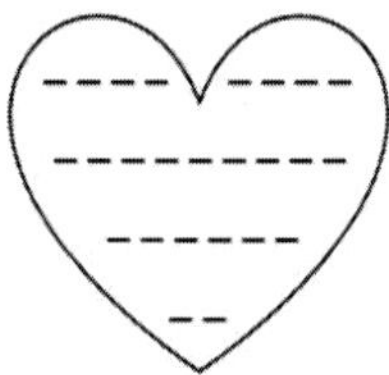

The test is to describe how the heart filled with minus signs becomes the heart filled with plus signs.

Most flunk.

Most people immediately reply that Jesus' death washed our sins away. In response, I erase the minus signs, leaving an empty heart. I then ask where the plus signs come from. Most don't know how to answer. Eventually some brave soul suggests they represent the good works of a Christian. If this is the case, however, then salvation is not a free gift because we have to do something to enter heaven.

The answer is the plus signs represent all the good works Jesus did in our behalf! Jesus wasn't our substitute only when he was on the cross. He was our stand-in his entire life. Galatians 4:4-5 indicates that Jesus came not only to die for us, but also to live for us. "But when the set time had fully come, God sent his Son, born of a woman, *born under the law, to redeem those under the law,* that we might receive adoption to sonship" (my emphasis).

It is instructive to compare this verse with another one in Galatians. In Galatians 3 Paul states that Jesus, through his death, *redeemed us from the curse of the law* (v. 13[26]). If redemption from the curse of the law was all that was needed, Paul could have stopped there. But in the verse

---

[26] Galatians 3:13 Christ redeemed us from the curse of the law by becoming a curse for us, for it is written: "Cursed is everyone who is hung on a pole."

quoted above he returns to the thought of redemption and talks about a different aspect. There he shows that Jesus, by placing himself under the law, *redeemed us from the obligations of the law.*

He did this by keeping the law perfectly for us. In his Sermon on the Mount Jesus said: "Do not think that I have come to abolish the Law or the Prophets; I have not come to abolish them but to fulfill them" (Matthew 5:17).

The exciting thing is we are now credited with his holiness. Note how Paul describes Jesus in the following passage. "It is because of him that you are in Christ Jesus, who has become for us wisdom from God – that is, our righteousness, holiness and redemption" (1 Corinthians 1:30). Jesus is our holiness! His perfect works are the plus signs in our hearts.

It's surprising that so many people fail my simple test. This indicates that the teaching of Jesus living a perfect life for us isn't stressed today. That's tragic. Ignorance of it increases the danger of people thinking they have to contribute to their salvation. Believers often, ever so subtly, look at their own works to see if they are right with God. How often, for example, haven't you heard believers wonder (or you yourself have wondered) if God still loves them because of some blatant sin they had committed. The flip side is feeling good about your status with God because of some good thing you did. In either case, people look at the wrong thing – they value their works and not

Christ's work. When we look at our own works we open ourselves up to many doubts.

Even worse things than doubts can develop from forgetting this important truth. If we, in any way, point to our own works as a reason why we qualify for heaven, we destroy the perfect case Jesus has made for us. Adding our imperfect works to Christ's masterpiece of perfection is like painting a tiny flower in the corner of a Rembrandt. It ruins the entire masterpiece. God knows we are inclined to do just that. This is why he *emphasizes* we are saved by Christ alone and not by our works. "For it is by grace you have been saved, through faith – and this is not from yourselves, it is the gift of God – not by works, so that no one can boast" (Ephesians 2:8-9).

When we remember that Jesus kept the law perfectly for us, we see the four Gospels in a wonderful new light. Far too often when people read about Jesus' life, they only see him as a perfect *example*. We are to love our enemies like he did. We are to be charitable like he was. It is true Jesus serves as an example but he mainly lived as our *substitute*. Viewing him this way makes reading the Gospels even more exciting. When I see Jesus being merciful, or loving his enemies, or spending the entire night in prayer, or witnessing fearlessly, or what have you – I realize I get the credit for what he did. Because he was living for me, I can put my name in his place! I can say I have loved my enemies because Jesus loved his enemies. I can say I am a fearless witness because Jesus was a fearless witness. Yes,

I can even say I am perfect because Jesus was perfect for me. He is my "righteousness, holiness and redemption" (1 Corinthians 1:30).

The Son of God gave his life not once but twice for us. As a result, he now freely offers us eternal life. "For the wages of sin is death, but *the gift of God is eternal life in Christ Jesus our Lord*" (Romans 6:23, my emphasis). God is the ultimate humanitarian.

For Further Reflection

1. We can't begin to imagine how hard it was for the Son of God to place himself under his own laws. Think of how difficult it would be for a father to follow the rules he established for his two-year old son. He couldn't go any place by himself. He would have to hold somebody's hand even when he climbed up a step. He would be told when and what to eat, when to sleep, what to wear, etc. This is a weak analogy of what Jesus did for us. And he did it not just a few days or even weeks. He did it for 33 years. His love for us is beyond all understanding.

2. Theologians label Jesus' satisfying God's commandments for us as his "active obedience." They then refer to his suffering and death for us as his "passive obedience." The Bible never uses these terms but they can be helpful if not pressed. There is no fine line between the two. For example, at his circumcision, Jesus not only obeyed God's command to be circumcised – an act which would be labeled active obedience; he also there shed his

blood for us – something which could be designated part of his passive obedience.

3. One of the most comforting phrases in the entire Bible is "for us." It highlights Jesus' substitutionary work. As you read the Bible, stay alert for it. You will be richly comforted as you remember Jesus both lived and died for you.

Chapter Ten: A Humanitarian by Dying for Us

"I'm stepping back so I don't get hit by the lightning bolt when it hits you!" How many times haven't you thought or said something similar when someone made an outrageous statement about God in your presence.

Obviously, we don't really think a lightning bolt will strike the person dead. This imagery does highlight, however, one important aspect of sin: it angers God. Sin is not just a spiritual cancer which wreaks havoc on the human race. It's not just a crime against God's law. Sin is also a personal affront to God, angering him immensely.

How greatly sin angers God can be seen at Christ's cross. There Jesus atoned for our sins. Many people don't feel the full force of that statement, however, because they have lost sight of the definition of "atone." It means *to appease a person's wrath*. On the cross Jesus appeased God's anger over our sins.

In other words, Christ's cross served as our lightning rod. There Jesus attracted all of God's anger at our sins. Wave after wave of God's anger washed over Jesus. Lightning bolt after lightning bolt struck Jesus. The Father didn't hold anything back. He unleashed on Jesus all his pent-up anger over human sin. Paul talks about that in Romans 3:25-26: "God presented Christ as a sacrifice of atonement, through the shedding of his blood – to be received by faith. He did this to demonstrate his righteousness, because in his forbearance he had left the sins committed beforehand unpunished – he did it to demonstrate his righteousness at the present time, so as to be just and the one who justifies those who have faith in Jesus." Because all of God's lightning bolts hit Jesus instead of us, all that remains for us is the glow and warmth of God's love.

The love which motivated God to punish Jesus is truly an out of this world love. Even if we remove sin from the equation, it would still be incomprehensible. The Creator dies for his creatures? The King dies for his subjects? It's supposed to be the other way around. But when we add sin back in, it truly becomes unfathomable. The King dying for his *rebellious* subjects? The Creator saving *creatures who he had declared worthless* (Romans 3:12[27])? This doesn't make any sense.

But that's the gospel truth. This is why God is the ultimate humanitarian.

The Bible uses the word grace for the unfathomable, unconditional, undeserved love God has for humanity. Some have taken each letter of "grace" to define it as:

---

[27] Romans 3:12 "All have turned away, they have together become worthless; there is no one who does good, not even one."

God's
Riches
At
Christ's
Expense

Consider what this meant to Christ. Centuries before Jesus was even born, the prophet Isaiah summed it up perfectly. "But he was pierced for our transgressions, he was crushed for our iniquities; the punishment that brought us peace was on him, and by his wounds we are healed. We all, like sheep, have gone astray, each of us has turned to our own way; and the Lord has laid on him the iniquity of us all" (Isaiah 53:5-6).

Two remarkable New Testament passages unfold what this entailed for Jesus. The first is Galatians 3:13: "Christ redeemed us from the curse of the law by becoming a curse for us, for it is written: 'Cursed is everyone who is hung on a pole.'" It would have been bad enough for Jesus to be cursed by his Father because of our sins. It's difficult enough to imagine the Father raining down curses on his Son. But Jesus wasn't just cursed by him; *he became a curse for us.* He so completely took our sins upon himself that he became a *curse personified.*

He also became *sin personified.* "God made him who had no sin to be sin for us" (2 Corinthians 5:21). In a very real way, by taking responsibility for the world's sin, Jesus became the world's greatest sinner. Even though the human race had no redeeming qualities, God was determined to redeem us. Therefore he covered Jesus with the awful stench of our sins. The shame and guilt of every horrific sin was superglued to Jesus. He became sin personified.

Remember what God told Moses when he approached the burning bush? "Take off your sandals, for the place where you are standing is holy ground" (Exodus 3:5). This is how I feel every time I read Jesus' cry from the cross: "My God, my God, why have you forsaken me?" (Matthew 27:46). This has to be one of the most profound statements ever uttered. With it Jesus pulls the curtain back ever so slightly to give us a glimpse of what it cost him to be our Savior.

It meant he was forsaken by his Father. It was nothing less than hell since the essence of hell is being driven from God's presence. Hell is what Jesus experienced on the cross. In fact, he had to experience it in order to save us. Hell is the punishment for sin and Jesus had to pay sin's full price. There were no discounts. There were no shortcuts. Jesus had to suffer hell as payment for our sins.

There is no way we can understand what this meant either to him or the Father. From all eternity, they had existed in perfect harmony. They were one God! There had never been even a whiff of friction between them. Now, there's not just friction, there's abandonment. The Father intentionally forsakes his Son. He curses him. He unleashes his white-hot wrath over mankind's sin on him. He shows him no mercy. Sacrifice seems too weak of a word to describe what the Father did for us. As somebody said, "The cross planted on Calvary's hill two thousand years ago was like a stake driven in the heart of God."

And the Son willingly takes it. His cry, "My God, my God" hints at how deeply he felt the Father's abandonment, since this is the only time Jesus ever addressed his Father with the more distant title of God. We also see the depth of the abandonment when he asks why. Some scholars believe Jesus' question shows that one aspect of his being forsaken was that, while he was suffering, the very knowledge of why he was suffering was withdrawn from him. I believe they are right because one aspect of hell is the absence of any hope.

Even though the Father abandoned him, Jesus didn't abandon the Father. Note again how he addresses his Father. "*My* God, *my* God."

The Father did all this to Jesus because he loves you. The Son suffered all this because he loves you. But God didn't just act for believers. "He [Jesus] is the atoning sacrifice for our sins, and not only for ours but also for the sins of the whole world" (1 John 2:2). Jesus' cross serves as the ultimate lightning rod *for all people*. Paul emphasized this when he wrote: "God was reconciling *the world* to himself in Christ, not counting people's sins against them" (2 Corinthians 5:19, my emphasis). It wasn't just believers whom God reconciled to himself – it was the world, it was everybody! It wasn't just believers' sins God forgave; it was everybody's sins.

This is astonishing. It underscores that God's message is not so much, "I will forgive you, ***if*** you believe in me." It is more, "I have forgiven you. Believe it." The difference between the two is significant. The second emphasizes how God forgives us proactively; how his forgiveness is not dependent on what we do; how salvation is *entirely his gift to us*. On the other hand, the first statement can easily cause people to think they must do something to be saved, thus creating doubt. The second statement is God-centered; the first can easily become self-centered.

Does the fact that God has already forgiven mankind make faith unimportant? No! Faith is absolutely essential. "For God so loved the world that he gave his one and only Son, *that whoever believes in him* shall not perish but have eternal life" (John 3:16, my emphasis). If people don't believe God has forgiven them, they won't enjoy the benefits of his forgiveness. They will continue to be afraid of God, angry at him, hiding from him. Their unbelief, however, doesn't change the basic fact that "God was reconciling the world to himself in Christ, not counting people's sins against them." This is why, in the last analysis, the only thing which damns people is unbelief.

One of the best ways we glorify God is by highlighting what happened at Jesus' crucifixion. There the Father unleashed on Jesus his divine wrath over all sin. There Jesus suffered hell for us. There he was abandoned by the Father. There Jesus completely paid for the sins of the world so that God no longer counts men's sins against them. There we see God in action as the ultimate humanitarian.

For Further Reflection

People sometimes wonder if it's proper to say God died for us. After all, God, by his very nature, can't die. But God dying for us is how the Bible talks. Paul wrote: "None of the rulers of this age understood it, for if they had, they would not have crucified *the Lord of glory*" (1 Corinthians 2:8, my emphasis). Peter told the Jews: "You killed *the author of life*" (Acts 3:15, my emphasis). "Lord of glory" and "author of life" are both titles for God.

This is not a minor point. Only God could pay for the sins of the whole world. As Psalm 49:7-8 states: "No one can redeem the life of another or give to God a ransom for them – the ransom for a life is costly, no payment is ever enough."

God can't die. God died for us. Both statements are biblically correct. Here is another place where God's ways are far above our ways (Isaiah 55:9[28]); where human reason must bow before God's revelation.

---

[28] Isaiah 55:9 "As the heavens are higher than the earth, so are my ways higher than your ways and my thoughts than your thoughts."

Chapter Eleven: A Humanitarian by Giving Us the Proof of Christ's Resurrection

Each of the four Gospels climaxes with Jesus' resurrection. The book of Acts shows it quickly became the heart and core of the apostles' teaching. "With great power the apostles continued to testify to the resurrection of the Lord Jesus" (Acts 4:33). The rest of the New Testament gives serious attention to it as well.

But did you realize the Bible describes Jesus' resurrection in two different ways? Sometimes it says he ***rose*** from the dead. "We believe that Jesus died and rose again" (1 Thessalonians 4:14). "Rose" emphasizes that Jesus accomplished it by his own power. Jesus stressed this very point during his ministry. "The reason my Father loves me is that I lay down my life – only to take it up again. No one takes it from me, but I lay it down of my own accord. I have authority to lay it down and authority to take it up again" (John 10:17-18). The fact that Jesus rose on his own authority is solid proof of his divinity. Paul, writing about Jesus, said: "*[he] was declared to be the Son of God* in power according to the Spirit of holiness *by his resurrection from the dead*, Jesus Christ our Lord" (Romans 1:4 [ESV[29]], my emphasis).

---

[29] ESV is the English Standard Version

The Bible also states Jesus ***was raised*** from the dead. "But God raised him from the dead" (Acts 2:24). The phrase "was raised" highlights the Father's action. It indicates that, by raising Jesus, he had accepted Jesus' payment for the world's sins. Jesus' resurrection was the Father's stamp of approval on his saving work. At the cross Jesus paid our debt. At Jesus' empty tomb God gives us our receipt marked "paid in full." Paul made this very point in Romans 4:25: "He was delivered over to death for our sins and was raised to life for our justification." Justification means *acquittal.* Jesus was raised because God had acquitted us. (We will take a more thorough look at this in chapter 12.)

These two different ways of describing Jesus' resurrection demonstrate that it is a proof of both his divinity and our salvation. Which one do you think the Bible emphasizes more?

Approximately 90% of the time it says he was raised! This alone demonstrates how determined God is to assure us Jesus has fully accomplished our salvation. He doesn't want us to have any doubts about it, even if it means putting less of the spotlight on Christ's divinity. This is how much he loves us.

Surprisingly, however, Jesus' resurrection does not serve only as a proof to believers. Speaking to the Athenians about Judgment Day, Paul said: "he [God] has set a day when he will judge the world with justice by the man he has appointed. *He has given proof of this to everyone by raising him from the dead*" (Acts 17:31, my emphasis). That Jesus' resurrection serves as proof, not just to people who view the Bible as God's Word, but *to everyone,* indicates it can be proven historically.

Whole books have been written on the subject. (One such book is Lee Strobel's *The Case for Christ.*) All I can give is a brief summary of how Jesus' resurrection can serve as a proof *to all people*. The key historical fact is the rapid spread of Christianity after Christ's resurrection. The two features making this so significant are:

- ➢ The rapid spread occurred in a very hostile environment.
- ➢ It was fueled by the proclamation of Christ's resurrection.

To better grasp the significance of these factors, I have created the following illustration. Imagine if less than two months after Lee Harvey Oswald assassinated President Kennedy, a new religion sprung up called "Oswaldites." Its proponents took out full page ads in major newspapers proclaiming that Lee Harvey Oswald had risen from the dead. Think of the uproar this would have caused. Also think of how easy it would have been to nip the movement in the bud by simply producing Oswald's body.

Even though this illustration is far-fetched, I hope you get the point. Such a scenario would have been similar to the situation which existed shortly after Jesus' resurrection. The apostles proclaimed the risen Christ in a very adverse setting. The people had demanded his crucifixion. Both the Jewish and Roman leaders had determined to kill him. Even if there wouldn't have been all that hostility, there would still have been great skepticism. The writings of the era reveal that people were just as incredulous of a bodily resurrection as unbelievers are today.

Just as in the case of Oswald, the easiest way for Jesus' enemies to destroy the new movement would have been by producing Jesus' body. But there is not even a hint in secular history of Jesus' body being found. Most critics of Christianity concede this point. They realize Jesus' tomb had to be empty.

Therefore they propose different theories trying to explain how the tomb became empty. Many of these theories are far-fetched like the swoon theory stating that Jesus didn't die. It claims he had only fainted and the cool of the tomb revived him. This, however, violates everything we know about Roman crucifixion. The Romans had procedures to make sure nobody survived being crucified (John 19:32-34[30]).

---

[30] John 19:32-34 The soldiers therefore came and broke the legs of the first man who had been crucified with Jesus, and then those of the other. But

The theory devised by the Jewish leaders immediately after the resurrection, namely, that the disciples stole the body, remains one of the more common explanations given (Matthew 28:11-15[31]). This explanation, however, makes no sense from the perspective of human nature. People lie either to cover up a wrong they had committed, or in order to gain something: fame, fortune, power, status, etc. From a human standpoint, the disciples lost everything and didn't gain anything from preaching a risen Lord. They were endlessly persecuted and eventually martyred. Why would they have persisted in the lie if it caused them nothing but grief? Why wouldn't they have turned state's evidence and reported where they had buried the body? That all the disciples kept the secret in the face of hardships and persecution, without even one breaking rank, is very difficult to believe.

For two thousand years, the enemies of Christianity have tried to come up with a plausible theory to explain Christ's empty tomb. None hold up under scrutiny. Only

---

when they came to Jesus and found that he was already dead, they did not break his legs. Instead, one of the soldiers pierced Jesus' side with a spear, bringing a sudden flow of blood and water.

[31] Matthew 28:11-15 While the women were on their way, some of the guards went into the city and reported to the chief priests everything that had happened. When the chief priests had met with the elders and devised a plan, they gave the soldiers a large sum of money, telling them, "You are to say, 'His disciples came during the night and stole him away while we were asleep.' If this report gets to the governor, we will satisfy him and keep you out of trouble." So the soldiers took the money and did as they were instructed. And this story has been widely circulated among the Jews to this very day.

the resurrection explains the tremendous change in the disciples. Only the resurrection explains their life-long devotion to spreading the news of the risen Lord. Only the resurrection explains the rapid spread of Christianity in a hostile environment. *The resurrection is a historical fact.* Timothy Keller, along with others, puts it even more strongly. He writes: "The resurrection of Jesus is a historical fact much more fully attested to than most other events of ancient history we take for granted."[32]

Because of his resurrection, faith in Jesus is not a leap in the dark. In his great love, God has given us Christ's resurrection as THE foundational fact on which we can base our faith. For this he deserves our endless worship as the ultimate humanitarian. "Praise be to the God and Father of our Lord Jesus Christ! In his great mercy he has given us new birth into a living hope through the resurrection of Jesus Christ from the dead, and into an inheritance that can never perish, spoil or fade" (1 Peter 1:3-4).

For Further Reflection

1. 1 Corinthians 15 is frequently labeled the "Great Resurrection Chapter." It reports that there were more than 500 eyewitnesses who saw the resurrected Lord

---

[32] Timothy Keller, *The Reason for God* (New York: Riverhead Books, 2008), p. 219.

(v. 6[33]) – many of whom were still alive when Paul wrote his letter to the Corinthians. In effect, Paul assured them that, if they had any doubts whether or not Jesus rose, there were hundreds of eyewitnesses they could ask. This is another example of how highly attested Jesus' resurrection was.

2. 1 Corinthians 15 also tells about the glorified resurrected bodies of believers. It compares corpses with seeds we plant. "But someone will ask, 'How are the dead raised? With what kind of body will they come?' How foolish! What you sow does not come to life unless it dies. When you sow, you do not plant the body that will be, but just a seed, perhaps of wheat or of something else" (1 Corinthians 15:35-37). Think, for example, about the tremendous difference between the acorn and the oak tree. This is how different our resurrected bodies will be from our present bodies! "So will it be with the resurrection of the dead. The body that is sown is perishable, it is raised imperishable; it is sown in dishonor, it is raised in glory; it is sown in weakness, it is raised in power" (1 Corinthians 15:42-43).

This is yet another instance of how God loves to give. He doesn't have to give us glorified bodies. But he wants to – because he is the ultimate humanitarian.

---

[33] 1 Corinthians 15:6 After that, he appeared to more than five hundred of the brothers and sisters at the same time, most of whom are still living, though some have fallen asleep.

3. Even though we will have glorified bodies, we won't lose our identities. At Jesus' transfiguration, the disciples immediately recognized Moses and Elijah (Matthew 17:4[34]). This hints at the possibility that one aspect of our heavenly bodies will be the ability to know people whom we have never met before.

---

[34] Matthew 17:4 Peter said to Jesus, "Lord, it is good for us to be here. If you wish, I will put up three shelters – one for you, one for Moses and one for Elijah."

Chapter Twelve: A Humanitarian by Giving Us a Wonderful Status

Many believers do not clearly differentiate between their *state* of sinning and their *status* before God. Clearly understanding the difference, however, can give great comfort.

For example, consider citizenship. Think of the difference it makes for immigrants to gain the status of citizens. I had a Vietnamese friend who served alongside Americans during the Vietnam War. After the war he came to live in the United States. Although he had lived here for many years, he refused to return to Vietnam to visit until he had gained American citizenship. Only then did he feel he would be protected. His *state* – how and where he lived – did not change. One legal document completely changed his *status*. It made a world of difference to him.

The same applies to believers. The Bible says they are now citizens of heaven. "But our citizenship is in heaven" (Philippians 3:20). Note the present tense "is." Even while believers are on earth, God already considers them citizens of heaven. This is a rich and wonderful thought, well worth dwelling on.

But I want to look at a different status the Bible has assigned believers, namely, that of "acquitted." It is the status the Bible highlights from beginning to end. Even though Scripture emphasizes it, many Christians don't understand or appreciate the assurance it gives.

One reason Christians often don't value this as highly as they could is because it is difficult to see in English translations. The Bible describes the status of "acquitted" with three words: *righteous*, *righteousness*, and *justify*. All three words come from the same Greek root word and are closely related, a fact impossible to see in English. We can make the connection between the three words by seeing that the literal meaning of the word translated justify is to declare righteous. Justify was a word commonly used to refer to a judge's verdict of righteous or *not guilty*. In other words, when the Bible says we are justified by faith in Jesus we should hear God, the judge of the universe, legally pronouncing us not guilty.

This is utterly amazing because we had committed so many crimes against God. We were serial sinners, repeating the same sins over and over. And we were serial sinners in regard to many sins. We sinned across the board. We were experts in a wide variety of sins.

What made matters even worse is that each sin is serious. Each is a capital crime. "The wages of sin is death" (Romans 6:23). Note how this statement is not limited to certain sins. The wages of each and every sin is death. When it comes to sin there are no misdemeanors.

Each and every sin made us guilty of shattering all of God's law. "For whoever keeps the whole law and yet stumbles at just one point is guilty of breaking all of it" (James 2:10). Even when we "stumble" – when we sin unintentionally – we are guilty.

Add all this up and we were guilty through and through. Sin had put us in a hopeless situation.

Until God stepped in. Even though we were guilty countless times over, he still justified us. He declared us righteous, pronouncing the verdict of not guilty over us. He did this solely because Jesus had already served our death sentence for us.

The point I want to highlight is how loving it was for God to not only do this, but to emphasize it. The most common biblical description of believers is not sinners or the guilty ones but the *righteous*, the *acquitted ones.* Over and over and over again, righteous is what God calls believers in his Word. In fact, he says it close to 180 times! It's obvious God doesn't want believers to have any doubts about their legal status. He wants them to know that they have been acquitted in the courtroom of heaven.

Think of how people react when a judge acquits them of a major crime. Cheers break out in the courtroom. Relief and joy wash over the face of the accused. Loved ones are hugged. Lawyers are congratulated. The acquitted throw their arms up in victory. They hold a victory party. They celebrate.

Now imagine how odd it would be, if instead of reacting with joy, they shuffled out of the courtroom with resigned looks and slumped shoulders. We would wonder if they heard the verdict correctly. "Didn't you hear you were found NOT guilty?"

Sadly, however, isn't this how many believers act? Instead of radiating joy, they appear burdened. They wallow in guilt. They doubt if God will forgive them. Thoughts of meeting their Maker fill them with anxiety rather than eager anticipation.

The problem is they have not distinguished between their *status* of not guilty and their *state* of sinning. Instead of focusing on their *status* of not guilty, they dwell on their *state* of sinning. Or they don't realize their *status* trumps their *state*. They forget that the most important thing is their legal status: that, in Christ, God has legally declared them not guilty.

The key, as it is in so many things, is to be Christ-centered. When we focus on our state, we are, in reality, being self-centered. In contrast, when we are fixated on our status, we are Christ-centered. It's obvious God wants us to lock on to our status. Otherwise he wouldn't have stressed it like he did. Because of our sin nature, however, concentrating on our status doesn't come naturally. We have to tenaciously work on remembering God has acquitted us.

Even here God helps us. The Holy Spirit lives within us as God's guarantee. "Now it is God who makes both us and you stand firm in Christ. He anointed us, set his seal of ownership on us, and put his Spirit in our hearts as a deposit, guaranteeing what is to come" (2 Corinthians 1:21-22). And while he is living within us, he regularly reminds us of who we are in Christ. "The Spirit himself testifies with our spirit that we are God's children" (Romans 8:16). God never wants us to forget our wonderful status!

Assured of our status, we can remain confident even when the reality of our sinfulness slaps us alongside our heads. Assured of our status, we can remain joyful even when we are disgusted by the sins we have committed.

And when we remember our divine acquittal, we can look forward to Judgment Day with great anticipation rather than great anxiety. We already know the verdict! We can approach Judgment Day like a defendant with an air-tight case. In fact, our case isn't just air-tight, it's perfect! Jesus who satisfied God's justice for us is the judge! He's not just our judge; the Bible also says he is our defense attorney! "But if anybody does sin, we have an advocate with the Father – Jesus Christ, the Righteous One" (1 John 2:1). When we put all these factors together, it is not a stretch to say Judgment Day will be the best day of our lives. It's the day God, the ultimate humanitarian, will acquit us before the entire world and welcome us into heaven with open arms!

For Further Reflection

1. Romans 4:25 addresses our justification in a unique way. Speaking about Jesus it says: "He was delivered over to death for our sins and was raised to life for our justification." The "for" in the phrases "for our sins" and "for our justification" means *because of.* That is how some translations, like the New American Standard Bible (NASB), translate it.

This is significant. Note the parallelism between the two parts of the verse. Just as our sins were the cause of Jesus' death, *our justification (acquittal) was the cause of his resurrection.*

To better understand this, think of Jesus' tomb as a prison. What is the message when a prisoner walks out the prison's front door? It tells the world he has served his sentence. God gave the world that very message when Jesus left his tomb. In this very striking way, he assured us that Jesus has fully served his sentence which, in reality, was our sentence. Romans 4:25 makes this point when it says Jesus "was raised to life for our justification." God raised Jesus from the dead and set him free from the prison of his tomb, because he had already acquitted us. If you ever wonder if God has actually declared you not guilty, revisit the Easter story and watch again as God releases Jesus from the prison of his tomb. See that and be convinced you are justified.

2. The Bible uses many other words to describe our wonderful status in Christ. Each one is rich in meaning. Many show that God did not only acquit us; he also adopted us. J. I. Packer put it this way, "Justification is the truly dramatic transition from the status of a condemned criminal awaiting a terrible sentence to that of an heir awaiting a fabulous inheritance."[35]

I have compiled a partial list of those words. (Since translations translate the words differently, the numbers behind each word will vary from translation to translation.) The important thing to see is the Bible describes believers, in the vast majority of cases, in a positive, even in an exalted way. The more we see ourselves as God sees us, the more we will glorify him in our words and actions.

Saints – 67 times
Holy – 36 times
Chosen – 23 times
Children of God – 13 times
Elect – 10 times
Heirs – 8 times
God's temple – 5 times

---

[35] J. I. Packer, *Knowing God* (Downers Grove, Illinois: Inter-Varsity Press, 1973), p. 121.

Chapter Thirteen: A Humanitarian by Giving Us Saving Faith

Jesus had done everything to bring us back to God. God had credited us with Jesus' death, wiping away our debt of sin. He also attributed Jesus' perfect obedience to us. One obstacle remained. We needed to believe in Jesus in order to enjoy the benefits of his perfect life and sacrificial death. "Whoever believes in him is not condemned, but whoever does not believe stands condemned already because they have not believed in the name of God's one and only Son" (John 3:18).

In Greek, the original language of the New Testament, "faith" and "believe" come from the same root word and are talking about the same thing. (Similar to "belief" and "believe.") They both emphasize trust. Biblical faith is more about the heart than the head. *It is more trusting than knowing*. It is the faith of a child.

There is also a vital distinction between general faith and *saving faith*. Saving faith is not a general belief in the existence of God. James shows the fallacy of such thinking. "You believe that there is one God. Good! Even the demons believe that – and shudder" (James 2:19). S*aving faith is specifically and solely trusting in Jesus' saving acts for us*. "So we, too, *have put our faith in Christ Jesus* that we may be justified *by faith in Christ* and not by the works of the law, because by the works of the law no one will be justified" (Galatians 2:16, my emphasis).

People with saving faith don't add any "ands" when they are asked why they are going to heaven. They don't say, "I'm going to heaven because Jesus died for me and I'm a good person." The only thing saving faith trusts in is Jesus' saving actions.

The problem is that nobody has the capability in and of themselves to trust in Jesus. Sin has so corrupted humanity that "there is no one who understands; *there is no one who seeks God.* All have turned away" (Romans 3:11-12, my emphasis). No one seeks God! By nature, everyone is spiritually blind (2 Corinthians 4:4[36]) and spiritually dead (Ephesians 2:1[37]). Because of the havoc sin has inflicted on the human race, no one, by themselves, can see the light and believe in Jesus.

Once again God had to step in and help us. 1 Corinthians 2:14 succinctly describes not only the problem but also the solution. "The person without the Spirit does not accept the things that come from the Spirit of God but considers them foolishness, and cannot understand them because they are discerned only through the Spirit." The faith we couldn't generate ourselves is

---

[36] 2 Corinthians 4:4 The god of this age has blinded the minds of unbelievers, so that they cannot see the light of the gospel that displays the glory of Christ, who is the image of God.

[37] Ephesians 2:1 As for you, you were dead in your transgressions and sins,

created in us by the Holy Spirit. "No one can say, 'Jesus is Lord,' except by the Holy Spirit" (1 Corinthians 12:3).

Faith itself is a gift of God! From beginning to end, salvation is entirely God's work. We contribute nothing. "For it is by grace you have been saved, through faith – and this is not from yourselves, it is the gift of God – not by works, so that no one can boast" (Ephesians 2:8-9). The "it" in the phrase "it is the gift of God" refers back to everything preceding it, *including faith.*

The various ways the Bible pictures conversion also emphasize that faith is something God gives people. No matter how it depicts conversion, God is the one actively working while people are the ones acted upon. Consider the following examples:

- "But because of his great love for us, God, who is rich in mercy, made us alive with Christ even when we were dead in transgressions – it is by grace you have been saved" (Ephesians 2:4-5).

- "He did not discriminate between us and them, for he purified their hearts by faith" (Acts 15:9).

- "For God, who said, 'Let light shine out of darkness,' made his light shine in our hearts to give us the light of the knowledge of God's glory displayed in the face of Christ" (2 Corinthians 4:6).

- "Yet to all who did receive him, to those who believed in his name, he gave the right to become children of God – children born not of natural descent, nor of human decision or a husband's will, but born of God" (John 1:12-13).

We were dead in sin. God made us alive. He purified our hearts by faith. And my favorite: just as his word created light from nothing in the beginning, so also his word creates the light of faith in our hearts from nothing. Even when John talks about receiving Jesus, he makes sure we know it happened not by human decision. It resulted from being born of God.

The Bible also emphasizes that faith itself is God's gift by how it describes Paul's conversion. No other person's conversion receives as much attention as his. The Bible records it in detail no less than three times (Acts 9:1-19; 22:1-16; 26:9-18). Not only this. Paul says his conversion was not the exception to the rule; *it was the rule itself.* "Here is a trustworthy saying that deserves full acceptance: Christ Jesus came into the world to save sinners – of whom I am the worst. But for that very reason I was shown mercy so that in me, the worst of sinners, Christ Jesus might display his immense patience *as an example for those who would believe in him* and receive eternal life" (1 Timothy 1:15-16, my emphasis).

If there was anybody who had no intention of trusting in Jesus, it was Paul! He was the early church's arch-enemy. He zealously persecuted Christians. He was dead in his sins and blind in his unbelief. If anyone fits the description of not seeking God, it was Paul. If anyone was actively resisting God, it was Paul. He was the least likely candidate to convert.

That is, if faith is something human-generated. Since it is a divine gift, however, bestowed on people whom God had judged as worthless (Romans 3:12[38]), Paul was no better or worse a candidate for conversion. Or to use another biblical picture, one person can't be deader than another. Dead is dead. Spiritually dead is spiritually dead.

So God stepped in and knocked Paul off his high horse, both literally and figuratively. Then he gave him both physical and spiritual sight. Paul contributed nothing to his conversion. From beginning to end, it was the work of God.

Over the years I have talked with many people who agonized over whether they truly believed. A common reason was they viewed coming to faith as something they had to do. They then wondered if they had done it correctly. Consider this finding from a survey of Christian college students. "The second most pervasive fear these students remembered was that they were 'not really saved.' No matter how many times they had 'asked Jesus to come into my heart' they were not positive that they had 'done

---

[38] Romans 3:12 "All have turned away, they have together become worthless; there is no one who does good, not even one."

it right.'"[39] Even though the survey was taken a number of years ago, the fear of not properly accepting Jesus remains a common one for many Christians.

By the way, just the act of worrying about whether you believe in Jesus or not is a sign of faith! This is not something an unbeliever would be concerned about.

Focusing on what the Bible has to say about faith as God's gift can remove many of those fears. It also gives God the credit for our faith – credit he so richly deserves. Even when it comes to faith, all glory goes to God, the ultimate humanitarian.

For Further Reflection

Repentance is a word closely associated with conversion, often being synonymous with it. This is seen in the fact that the command to repent is most commonly addressed to unbelievers. It is important to keep in mind the truth of 2 Corinthians 4:6[40] and the comparison it draws between God speaking at creation and conversion. Just as God's command "let there be light" created light, so also God's command to repent creates repentance in a person's heart.

---

[39] Mickelsen, Alvera, *Healthy & Unhealthy Fear of the Lord*, Leadership, Spring 1985, p.83

[40] 2 Corinthians 4:6 For God, who said, "Let light shine out of darkness," made his light shine in our hearts to give us the light of the knowledge of God's glory displayed in the face of Christ.

The Greek word most commonly used for repentance literally means *a change of mind.* It describes the God-worked paradigm shift in people from trusting in their works to trusting in Christ's saving works. *Its essence is a new mindset. Its fruit are new works.* It is vitally important to keep a clear distinction between the essence of faith and/or repentance on one hand, and their fruits on the other hand. We will look at this more in depth in chapter 18.

One of the most prominent fruits of repentance is joy. This is exemplified by Zacchaeus, the repentant tax-collector. His story is told in Luke 19:1-10[41]. What does he do? Without any coercion or even a hint of a suggestion from Jesus, he joyfully gives half of his wealth to the poor. How could he not be joyful? He now knew Jesus had saved him fully and freely.

---

[41] Luke 19:1-10 Jesus entered Jericho and was passing through. A man was there by the name of Zacchaeus; he was a chief tax collector and was wealthy. He wanted to see who Jesus was, but because he was short he could not see over the crowd. So he ran ahead and climbed a sycamore-fig tree to see him, since Jesus was coming that way. When Jesus reached the spot, he looked up and said to him, "Zacchaeus, come down immediately. I must stay at your house today." So he came down at once and welcomed him gladly. All the people saw this and began to mutter, "He has gone to be the guest of a sinner." But Zacchaeus stood up and said to the Lord, "Look, Lord! Here and now I give half of my possessions to the poor, and if I have cheated anybody out of anything, I will pay back four times the amount." Jesus said to him, "Today salvation has come to this house, because this man, too, is a son of Abraham. For the Son of Man came to seek and to save the lost."

Chapter Fourteen: A Humanitarian by Giving Us the Gospel

In Romans 10:14 Paul asks three rhetorical questions. "How, then, can they call on the one they have not believed in? And how can they believe in the one of whom they have not heard? And how can they hear without someone preaching to them?" The obvious answer to all three questions is they can't. They can't believe in someone they have never heard of, and they can't hear without someone preaching to them. Paul drives the point home when he concludes: "Consequently, faith comes from hearing the message, and the message is heard through the word about Christ" (Romans 10:17). In order to be brought to faith, people need to be connected with the "word about Christ" or, as it is more commonly called, the gospel.

Paul had already made this point earlier in his letter to the Romans: "I am not ashamed of the gospel, because *it is the power of God that brings salvation to everyone who believes:* first to the Jew, then to the Gentile" (Romans 1:16, my emphasis). The gospel brings salvation to *everyone* who believes. Not just some. Everyone. It is not just *a power* of God imparting salvation. It is *the power.* The Holy Spirit uses the gospel and *only* the gospel to create faith.

Because the gospel plays such a vital role, it is essential to be clear on what it is. The word gospel literally means *good news*. The Bible uses it to describe the *very specific message of Jesus' saving works for us*. Its focus is entirely on God's love for us. It talks about what Jesus has already done on our behalf and excludes any thought of human contribution to salvation. Its message is DONE, not do. It announces that God forgives us freely and fully in Jesus. It is the best news of all!

As Paul stated, it is not only great news. It is also a tremendously powerful message. This underscores the amazing truth that the gospel is a creative word containing the very power to bring to pass what it commands. When Jesus stood before Lazarus' tomb, his command to come out gave Lazarus new life. Obviously Lazarus didn't have the ability to obey Jesus' command. He was dead! It was Jesus' word which brought him to life. In a similar way the Holy Spirit, through the gospel, calls out to unbelievers to believe. Like Lazarus, they don't have the ability to obey any command – including the command to believe. They can't obey because they are spiritually dead. But just like Jesus' command created life in Lazarus, so also the gospel creates life in unbelievers. Paul simply says: "By this gospel you are saved" (1 Corinthians 15:2).

The fact that people can only come to faith through the gospel underscores the importance of believers spreading the great news. The above passages rule out the possibility of the Holy Spirit bringing people to faith without their coming into contact with the gospel. I want to highlight this fact because many believers, without much thought:

- Comfort themselves with the unfounded idea that the Holy Spirit will save people even if they have never heard the gospel.

- Think God will give people another chance to believe after they die. Along with passages like Hebrews 9:27[42], Jesus' story about the rich man and poor Lazarus (Luke 16:19-31[43]) rules out this possibility.

If either of these two viewpoints were true, then there wouldn't be much urgency to do mission work. If they

---

[42] Hebrew 9:27 Just as people are destined to die once, and after that to face judgment,

[43] Luke 16:19-31 "There was a rich man who was dressed in purple and fine linen and lived in luxury every day. At his gate was laid a beggar named Lazarus, covered with sores and longing to eat what fell from the rich man's table. Even the dogs came and licked his sores. The time came when the beggar died and the angels carried him to Abraham's side. The rich man also died and was buried. In Hades, where he was in torment, he looked up and saw Abraham far away, with Lazarus by his side. So he called to him, 'Father Abraham, have pity on me and send Lazarus to dip the tip of his finger in water and cool my tongue, because I am in agony in this fire.' But Abraham replied, 'Son, remember that in your lifetime you received your good things, while Lazarus received bad things, but now he is comforted here and you are in agony. And besides all this, between us and you a great chasm has been set in place, so that those who want to go from here to you cannot, nor can anyone cross over from there to us.' He answered, 'Then I beg you, father, send Lazarus to my family, for I have five brothers. Let him warn them, so that they will not also come to this place of torment.' Abraham replied, 'They have Moses and the Prophets; let them listen to them.' 'No, father Abraham,' he said, 'but if someone from the dead goes to them, they will repent.' He said to him, 'If they do not listen to Moses and the Prophets, they will not be convinced even if someone rises from the dead.'"

were true, then it wasn't wise for Paul and the other apostles to sacrifice their lives telling others about Jesus. If they were true, then countless missionaries down through the centuries have wasted their lives spreading the gospel.

Paul and all those missionaries weren't wrong. In various ways the Bible emphasizes how essential it is to share the gospel. The passages quoted above create the urgency to spread it. The risen Lord made sharing the gospel a high priority when he told his disciples: "Go into all the world and preach the gospel to all creation" (Mark 16:15). The book of Acts underscores the importance of spreading the word with its reporting of the early church's efforts to tell others about Jesus. There is no question: believers are to share the gospel.

One thing often lost in this discussion is the great love God shows believers by calling them to be his witnesses. Far too often, Christians view sharing the message of Christ as a burden rather than as a blessing. Some approach it with fear rather than joy. They fail to see what a tremendous privilege God has given them – that he considers them nothing less than his ambassadors. "He has committed to us the message of reconciliation. We are therefore Christ's ambassadors, as though God were making his appeal through us" (2 Corinthians 5:19-20).

Stop and think about the great honor it is to be an ambassador for the King of the universe. We become co-workers with God himself (2 Corinthians 6:1[44]). Reflect on the tremendous message God has entrusted to you. Don't ever forget how essential it is for people to hear it. Believe that it is the most powerful word in the world and that it will *always* accomplish something (Isaiah 55:10-11[45]).

There's still more. The glorious, all-powerful, risen Lord has promised to be with us every step of the way! "Then Jesus came to them and said, 'All authority in heaven and on earth has been given to me. Therefore go and make disciples of all nations, baptizing them in the name of the Father and of the Son and of the Holy Spirit, and teaching them to obey everything I have commanded you. *And surely I am with you always, to the very end of the age*'" (Matthew 28:18-20, my emphasis).

As the ultimate humanitarian, God has not only given us the gospel for our own salvation; he has also given us the exalted task and privilege of sharing it with people who desperately need to hear it. You can be used by God to make the difference in somebody's eternal destiny! There is no more rewarding work than that.

---

[44] 2 Corinthians 6:1 As God's co-workers we urge you not to receive God's grace in vain.

[45] Isaiah 55:10-11 As the rain and the snow come down from heaven, and do not return to it without watering the earth and making it bud and flourish, so that it yields seed for the sower and bread for the eater, so is my word that goes out from my mouth: It will not return to me empty, but will accomplish what I desire and achieve the purpose for which I sent it.

For Further Reflection

1. People often put undue pressure on themselves when they share the gospel. They see themselves as lawyers rather than as witnesses. There's a big difference between the two. A witness testifies to what he knows. A lawyer then uses the witness' testimony to try and convince people. It is the Holy Spirit's job to convince people Jesus is the Savior. He is the lawyer. We are only the witnesses. Our job is to tell what we know. His job is to convert.

2. Some people think they must be a biblical expert before they can witness. Although it is important to grow in biblical knowledge, it is also important to stick to the basics when first introducing people to Jesus. We need to trust the power of the simple gospel. This is what Paul did when he came to Corinth. Being Greek, the Corinthians had a high regard for human wisdom. Even though Paul was highly educated, he stuck to the basics. "So it was with me, brothers and sisters. When I came to you, I did not come with eloquence or human wisdom as I proclaimed to you the testimony about God. For I resolved to know nothing while I was with you except Jesus Christ and him crucified" (1 Corinthians 2:1-2). Paul says he *resolved* to focus on "Jesus Christ and him crucified." He made a conscious effort not to go beyond the basics when he first shared Christ with them. This is a good strategy for all to follow.

3. The word "dynamite" is derived from the Greek word translated as "power" in Romans 1:16. When you

share the gospel, picture yourself placing a stick of dynamite alongside their stony heart of unbelief. It's then up to the Holy Spirit to light the fuse in his timing and choosing (John 3:8[46]).

The word "dynamo" is also derived from that Greek word. A dynamo doesn't give a blast of power like dynamite. It is a generator producing a constant stream of energy. The gospel is the dynamo generating the energy needed to lead a God-pleasing life. The more we focus on what Jesus has done for us, the more energized we are to show him our thanks with godly living. Many believers, however, focus almost entirely on Bible passages which describe a godly life. Those Scriptures tell us what a godly life consists of, but they don't empower us to live them. Only the gospel generates the power for Christian living. We need to be regularly connected to our gospel generator.

---

[46] John 3:8 "The wind blows wherever it pleases. You hear its sound, but you cannot tell where it comes from or where it is going. So it is with everyone born of the Spirit."

Chapter Fifteen: A Humanitarian by Giving Us Baptism

In the last chapter, we saw how the Bible stresses that the Holy Spirit creates faith only by means of the gospel. In light of this truth, the following two Bible verses about being *born again* are intriguing:

- "You have been *born again*, not of perishable seed, but of imperishable, through the living and enduring word of God" (1 Peter 1:23, my emphasis).

- "Jesus replied, 'Very truly I tell you, no one can see the kingdom of God unless they are *born again.*' 'How can someone be born when they are old?' Nicodemus asked. 'Surely they cannot enter a second time into their mother's womb to be born!' Jesus answered, 'Very truly I tell you, no one can enter the kingdom of God unless they are born of water and the Spirit. Flesh gives birth to flesh, but the Spirit gives birth to spirit'" (John 3:3-6, my emphasis).

Or consider these two passages about *salvation*:

- "God was pleased through the foolishness of what was preached to *save* those who believe" (1 Corinthians 1:21, my emphasis).

- "In it only a few people, eight in all, were saved through water, and this water symbolizes baptism that now *saves* you also – not the removal of dirt from the body but the pledge of a clear conscience toward God" (1 Peter 3:20-21, my emphasis).

In a little while, we will take a closer look at John 3:3-6 and 1 Peter 3:20-21. Now I want to emphasize that the Bible ascribes the same actions ("saving" and "born again") to both the word and baptism. This teaches a profound truth. *The one, saving, Spirit-filled gospel is offered in two forms: the word and baptism.* It's comparable to a pipe delivering water to our homes. It branches out so we can access the water from various outlets. It doesn't matter which outlet we use. We receive the same water.

God has done something similar. In his tremendous love, he has designated the two outlets of word and baptism for his saving gospel. As with the water coming into the house, they both convey the very same powerful, life-giving gospel.

This also underscores that *baptism is a divine activity and not a human work*. God works a spiritual birth through baptism. He uses it to save. We see the same phenomenon in the verses dealing with baptism as we do in those describing conversion. *God is the one doing the work. People are the ones who are worked on*. Romans 6:3-4 is representative. "Don't you know that all of us who were baptized into Christ Jesus were baptized into his death? We were therefore buried with him through baptism into death in order that, just as Christ was raised from the dead through the glory of the Father, we too may live a new life." Note the passive verbs: "were baptized into his death," "were buried with him." God baptized us into Jesus' death. God buried us with Jesus in baptism. God raised us to a new life. Or consider Ephesians 5:26 which talks about the cleansing power of baptism: "to make her holy, cleansing her by the washing with water through the word."

I repeat: baptism is a divine activity, not a human work. Being baptized is no more a work than reading the Bible. Baptism is a place where the Holy Spirit works.

Let's now take a closer look at John 3:3-6. The critical phrase is "unless they are born of water and the Spirit." Does it describe one or two births? Grammar gives us the answer. We need to remember this was originally written in Greek. In Greek the single use of the word "of" is significant. It combines the water and Spirit into one birth. If Jesus wanted to specify two distinct births he would have had to repeat the word "of" (unless they are born of water and *of* the Spirit). F. Dale Bruner, one of the world's preeminent biblical scholars, explains: "Water and the gift of the Spirit cannot be more closely connected than they are in John 3:5: 'of water *and* the Spirit.' John does not place a second 'of' (*ex*) before 'Spirit' as he would if he were describing two different events. The single *ex* describes the single occasion. This singularity is then completely established by the *aorist* subjunctive passive *gennethe* which means literally '*once* born' of water and Spirit."[47]

In coming to a correct understanding of this passage, it is also helpful to know that the Jews were very familiar with ceremonial washings. Later in John 3, we see a dispute over such washings (John 3:25[48]). Sometimes, as in Hebrews 9:10[49], these washings were also called baptisms (the word translated "ceremonial washings" is the Greek word for baptism). In John 3 Jesus tells Nicodemus about a baptism which wasn't ceremonial, but one giving new life because it was a baptism of water and Spirit!

Before leaving John 3:3-6, one additional point needs to be addressed. Jesus' statement, "no one can enter the kingdom of God unless they are born of water and the Spirit," seems to indicate that baptism is essential for salvation. Here too we need to keep in mind the historical context. Nicodemus was a Pharisee (John 3:1[50]). Luke 7:30 reports that "the Pharisees and the experts in the law rejected God's purpose for themselves, because they had

---

[47] F. Dale Bruner, *A Theology of the Holy Spirit* (Grand Rapids, Michigan: Eerdmans Publishing, 1970), p. 257f.

[48] John 3:25 An argument developed between some of John's disciples and a certain Jew over the matter of ceremonial washing.

[49] Hebrew 9:10 They are only a matter of food and drink and various ceremonial washings – external regulations applying until the time of the new order.

[50] John 3:1 Now there was a Pharisee, a man named Nicodemus who was a member of the Jewish ruling council.

not been baptized by John." Baptism had become a flashpoint with the Pharisees. They refused to be baptized. Because they took this stand, it was only natural for Jesus to stress to a Pharisee the need to be baptized.

The rest of Scripture, while emphasizing baptism's importance, does not say it is essential for salvation. Mark 16:16 is representative. "Whoever believes and is baptized will be saved, but whoever does not believe will be condemned." The lack of faith, not the lack of baptism, is what condemns people.

1 Peter 3:18-21[51] also merit a few words of explanation. In the preceding verses, Peter talks about the flood and how Noah's family was saved in the ark. He then somewhat unexpectedly turns to baptism. His words are both clear and breathtaking. He doesn't say the waters of baptism are a symbol. He says the waters of the flood symbolize baptism. He then proceeds to clearly state that baptism saves. It saves, Peter says, by giving a clear conscience before God. The only way our consciences can be clear is by knowing Jesus has washed all our sins away.

---

[51] 1 Peter 3:18-21 For Christ also suffered once for sins, the righteous for the unrighteous, to bring you to God. He was put to death in the body but made alive in the Spirit. After being made alive, he went and made proclamation to the imprisoned spirits – to those who were disobedient long ago when God waited patiently in the days of Noah while the ark was being built. In it only a few people, eight in all, were saved through water, and this water symbolizes baptism that now saves you also – not the removal of dirt from the body but the pledge of a clear conscience toward God. It saves you by the resurrection of Jesus Christ,

In other words, baptism saves because the Holy Spirit uses it to work faith, thus producing a clear conscience.

In many cases a person will be saved, or born again, by hearing or reading the Word. (Remember there is one saving gospel but two different outlets. No matter what outlet people use, they receive the same powerful, Spirit-filled gospel.) This doesn't mean, however, that such people gain nothing from baptism. It becomes another wonderful way for them to receive God's forgiveness and acceptance. At Pentecost Peter first preached to the crowd. He then said: "Repent and be baptized, every one of you, in the name of Jesus Christ *for the forgiveness of your sins.* And you will receive the gift of the Holy Spirit" (Acts 2:38, my emphasis).

There is, however, one group whose initial contact with the gospel is usually through baptism. I'm talking about infants. The Holy Spirit has used baptism to create saving faith in millions of babies. This is something they desperately need since they are sinful from conception (see chapter 3). As sinners, they also fall under God's condemnation. "Just as one trespass resulted in condemnation *for all people*" (Romans 5:18, my emphasis). It is clear. There are no exceptions to this condemnation.

And babies can believe, since faith is something the Holy Spirit creates in people's hearts rather than something they generate themselves. Obviously God can create faith in infants. This is evident in how Jesus talks about infants praising God, an act which implies faith.

"Have you never read, 'From the lips of children and infants you, Lord, have called forth your praise'" (Matthew 21:16).

Jesus also spoke about the faith of very small children. After placing a small child before his disciples, Jesus said: "If anyone causes *one of these little ones – those who believe in me* – to stumble, it would be better for them to have a large millstone hung around their neck and to be drowned in the depths of the sea" (Matthew 18:6, my emphasis).

It is always important to remember that faith is essentially trust. Even though a newborn baby hasn't any concept of "mother," he knows when his mother holds him and is comforted. He "trusts" his mother. In the same way, infants can "trust" in Jesus even though they don't have a concept of "Savior." The key is to connect them with the life-saving gospel.

Before ascending into heaven, our risen Lord gave the church its marching orders. "Go and make disciples of all nations, baptizing them in the name of the Father and of the Son and of the Holy Spirit, and teaching them to obey everything I have commanded you" (Matthew 28:19-20). Here we see the twin outlets of the gospel in "baptizing" and "teaching." There we also see no one is excluded. "All nations" includes everybody regardless of race, gender, or *age*.

Baptism, along with his word, is another wonderful gift from God, the ultimate humanitarian.

For Further Reflection

1. Our English words baptize and baptism are *transliterated* from the Greek. This simply means we took these words directly from the Greek and made them English words. A modern example of transliteration is fiesta which is taken directly from Spanish.

Many people think the word "baptize" means to immerse. The Bible, however, uses it in contexts where it simply means to wash. In Hebrews 9:10, for example, the word "washings" translates the Greek word baptism. "They are only a matter of food and drink and various ceremonial washings – external regulations applying until the time of the new order." We know that most of those ceremonial washings did not involve immersion, only a sprinkling of water.

What is critical in baptism is applying water in the name of the Triune God. Even though immersion symbolizes the spiritual burial and resurrection described in Romans 6, it is not essential.

2. Many people have questions on 1 Corinthians 15:29. "Now if there is no resurrection, what will those do who are baptized for the dead? If the dead are not raised at all, why are people baptized for them?" Sometimes we have to admit that we don't know what a specific passage refers to, even though it was clear to the original recipients. This is one of those cases.

We can also be clear, however, *on what it is does not say*. Paul never says believers participated in the practice of baptisms for the dead. In fact, he seems to be emphasizing a contrast between the people described in verse 29 and believers. He continues in verse 30 by saying, "And as for us" and then addresses his readers with "you" in verse 31.

Even if verse 29 refers to a group of believers, it only describes what some did. The Bible never *commands* baptisms for the dead.

Furthermore, other biblical passages rule out any interpretation which says being baptized in the name of a deceased person helps the person in any way. Once a person dies, they immediately face judgment. "Just as people are destined to die once, and after that to face judgment" (Hebrews 9:27).

I have read over fifty different interpretations of this verse. Much of it centers on the Greek preposition translated "for." It can also mean "over." Some commentators think people were baptized over the graves of their loved ones to indicate they believed they would be reunited with them at the resurrection. That is just one of many such interpretations. The bottom line is that we don't exactly know what Paul is referring to.

Chapter Sixteen: A Humanitarian by Giving Us His Supper

Think of a time when you sinned against a loved one. You felt terrible. You begged for their forgiveness. And they forgave you. Was that the last time you mentioned it to them? I highly doubt it. More than likely you apologized repeatedly. You needed to hear them reassuring you all was good.

It's not easy letting go of guilt. Guilt can superglue itself to our consciences. It can permeate and contaminate every waking thought. It often takes more than one word of forgiveness to erase it.

The Lord knows this. That is why he has filled the Bible with clear statements assuring us we are completely forgiven in Christ. Sometimes, however, we need even more. Think of the added comfort we receive when the person we have wronged not only tells us they have forgiven us, but then accompanies those words with a warm hug.

In a way, his supper is how God hugs us and tells us we are forgiven. In biblical times, sharing a meal was a significant act of fellowship. This is why the Pharisees were shocked when Jesus ate with "sinners." By inviting us to his table, the Lord is reassuring us that all is good between him and us.

This, however, is just the beginning. His supper is so much more. Jesus indicated that by how he spoke of it. The Bible records the words Jesus used to institute the supper in four different places. As we look at the different accounts, we encounter something especially fascinating. They reveal that Jesus talked about the wine in two different ways. Matthew and Mark record Jesus describing it as "my blood of the covenant." (Mark 14:24: "This is my blood of the covenant, which is poured out for many.") Luke and Paul, however inform us that Jesus also called it, "the new covenant in my blood." (Luke 22:20: "This cup is the new covenant in my blood, which is poured out for you.")

This isn't sloppy reporting. This is God's inspired word. Both phrases were significant to the Jews of Jesus' day. They are Old Testament expressions used in the context of *forgiveness*. By using them to describe his supper, Jesus emphasized how special it is: it conveys God's forgiveness.

Let's first consider the phrase, "the new covenant in my blood." It is from Jeremiah 31:31-34. As you read these verses, note that they contain no "ifs." The new covenant is unilateral. (See chapter 4.) It is entirely about what the Lord will do and is not dependent on what people will do.

> "The days are coming," declares the LORD, "when I will make *a new covenant* with the people of Israel and with the people of Judah. It will not

> be like the covenant I made with their ancestors when I took them by the hand to lead them out of Egypt, because they broke my covenant, though I was a husband to them," declares the LORD. "This is the covenant I will make with the people of Israel after that time," declares the LORD. "I will put my law in their minds and write it on their hearts. I will be their God, and they will be my people. No longer will they teach their neighbor, or say to one another, 'Know the LORD,' because they will all know me, from the least of them to the greatest," declares the LORD. "For *I will forgive their wickedness and will remember their sins no more.*" (Jeremiah 31:31-34, my emphasis)

The Greek word for covenant was also used to describe a person's last will and testament. For example, Hebrews 9:16-17 utilizes it that way. "In the case of a will, it is necessary to prove the death of the one who made it, because a will is in force only when somebody has died; it never takes effect while the one who made it is living." (The word translated "will" is the same Greek word translated "covenant" in Luke 22:20.)

Viewing Jesus' supper as the specific covenant of a last will and testament is instructive. As the Hebrews passage points out, a will is put into force at a person's death. Less than 24 hours after instituting his supper, Jesus died.

Think back to the scenario at the beginning of the chapter. Envision yourself as having sinned grievously against a loved one who has written you into their will. In such a situation, you can easily imagine reading the will more than once to be reassured that you are still in it.

Partaking of his supper is like this. There my Lord declares that the new covenant of forgiveness still applies to me. He tells me I am still in his will – I am still an heir of heaven. I remain an heir because he paid for all my sins with his blood.

The other phrase Jesus used, "my blood of the covenant," reinforces this thought. It comes from the time when God ratified his covenant with Israel at Mt. Sinai. The book of Hebrews explains its significance. "When Moses had proclaimed every command of the law to all the people, he took the blood of calves, together with water, scarlet wool and branches of hyssop, and sprinkled the scroll and all the people. He said, '*This is the blood of the covenant*, which God has commanded you to keep.' In the same way, he sprinkled with the blood both the tabernacle and everything used in its ceremonies. In fact, the law requires that *nearly everything be cleansed with blood*, and *without the shedding of blood there is no forgiveness*" (Hebrews 9:19-22, my emphasis).

At Mt. Sinai, God signed and sealed the covenant with blood sprinkled on individual Israelites. Think of how they must have felt as the blood trickled down their faces. In this striking way, each was assured they were included in the covenant.

In a similar way, Jesus signed and sealed the new covenant with his own blood. Our eyes see the bread and wine. Our hands touch it. Our mouths taste it. In this most intimate way, Jesus impresses upon each participant that his blood has cleansed them – that they are forgiven. "This is my blood of the covenant, which is poured out for many *for the forgiveness of sins*" (Matthew 26:28, my emphasis).

His supper is a most precious gift from God. Participation in it is not about me sending a message to God. Or about renewing my covenant with God. It's not about what I do at all. It's all about Jesus confirming for me, in a most wonderful way, that his new covenant of forgiveness applies personally to me.

Because it is so precious, God warns us to handle it very carefully. "So then, whoever eats the bread or drinks the cup of the Lord in an unworthy manner will be guilty of sinning against the body and blood of the Lord. Everyone ought to examine themselves before they eat of the bread and drink from the cup. For those who eat and drink without discerning the body of Christ eat and drink judgment on themselves. That is why many among you are weak and sick, and a number of you have fallen asleep" (1 Corinthians 11:27-30).

These are sobering words. Some people even fell asleep (i.e. died) because they ate and drank in an unworthy manner! The stakes are this high! It is vital, therefore, to see exactly what constitutes eating and drinking unworthily.

Thankfully we are not left guessing. "For those who eat and drink *without discerning the body of Christ* eat and drink judgment on themselves" (my emphasis). The context reveals the reason the Corinthians weren't discerning Christ's body: they were drunk. It's significant, however, that Paul broadens the warning to include more than drunkenness. The underlying principle is that unworthy partaking, regardless of the reason, results from not recognizing Christ's body as present in the supper.

Paul had already laid the foundation for this in 1 Corinthians 10 when he talks about the miraculous union of Christ's body and blood with the bread and wine. "Is not the cup of thanksgiving for which we give thanks a participation in the blood of Christ? And is not the bread that we break a participation in the body of Christ?" (v. 16). Paul talks about two participations: one between the cup (wine) and Christ's blood and another between the bread and Christ's body. The Greek word translated participation is *koinonia*. It describes a close, intimate union. The bread and wine do not just symbolize Christ's body and blood. They participate, are united, with the body and blood.

I will be the first to admit I can't comprehend this. In a wonderful, miraculous way, all four elements (bread, wine, body, blood) are present. I don't understand it, but I surely appreciate it. This shows me how much Jesus loves me. He goes to these great lengths to reassure me of his forgiveness. That he would do so really shouldn't surprise me. He can do anything. And he is, after all, the ultimate humanitarian.

For Further Reflection

1. In 1 Corinthians 11:28[52], Paul says that everyone should examine themselves. People need to understand what the supper is before partaking of it. This naturally excludes unbelievers. But not just unbelievers. People not only need the mental capacity to be able to examine themselves, they also need to be taught about the supper. Ignorance is not bliss when it comes to participating in Jesus' supper.

2. As was already mentioned, the supper is a fellowship meal. It not only unites us with Christ in a wonderful way, it also unites us wonderfully with the other participants. In the context of the supper Paul wrote: "Because there is one loaf, we, who are many, are one body, for we all share the one loaf" (1 Corinthians 10:17).

This is a wonderful bond. For example, on occasion, when counseling married couples who wanted to reconcile with each other, I have had them take his supper together. As they stood before the Lord's altar, being reassured of his forgiveness, they often became motivated and empowered to forgive each other.

---

[52] 1 Corinthians 11:28 Everyone ought to examine themselves before they eat of the bread and drink from the cup.

Chapter Seventeen: A Humanitarian by Giving Us Prayer

Isn't it amazing that one of the most common activities of a believer is praying? We pray so frequently, however, we often fail to see how awesome a privilege prayer truly is. It is another outstanding gift from the ultimate humanitarian.

In prayer, we have *direct* access to the king of the universe himself! Think of how honored we would be if the president of the United States gave us the number to his private line. I doubt if any of us could imagine this ever happening. Let's not even aim that high. We are often thrilled to get the direct line to anybody in authority: whether it is the CEO of a company or the mayor of a town.

In prayer we have direct access to the king of the universe himself!

And we have *unlimited* access. We don't have to work through a maze of automated menu choices. We don't have to speak commands to a computer which misinterprets everything we say. We don't have to explain our problem over and over to a series of assistants. We never hear a busy signal. We are never put on hold. Each and every prayer is heard and answered by God himself! This truly is mind-boggling.

If we were talking about a business, we would be raving about its fantastic customer service. This, however, is about so much more. This is about the all-powerful, all-majestic king of the universe granting us the opportunity to talk with him *at any time*.

Not only does he give us the opportunity, he encourages us to make good use of it. “Cast all your anxiety on him because he cares for you” (1 Peter 5:7). God is not reluctant to listen to us. Instead he urges us to bring *everything* to him in prayer.

And he promises to answer all our prayers. “Call on me in the day of trouble; I will deliver you, and you will honor me” (Psalm 50:15). “Ask and it will be given to you; seek and you will find; knock and the door will be opened to you” (Matthew 7:7).

Obviously he doesn’t answer every prayer with a yes. But that doesn’t mean he hasn’t answered the prayer. He lovingly and patiently listens to each and every prayer. Then he answers, according to his perfect wisdom and motivated by his perfect love. His answer is perfect!

Prayer is an awesome gift from the ultimate humanitarian – *for believers.*

Praying is a privilege of believers, not a human right. The Lord rejects the prayers of those who pray to him without listening to him. “If anyone turns a deaf ear to my instruction, even their prayers are detestable" (Proverbs 28:9). "'When I called, they did not listen; so when they called, I would not listen,' says the LORD Almighty" (Zechariah 7:13).

This is why Jesus taught us to pray in his name (John 14:14[53]). He wasn't establishing a wooden rule insisting that every prayer must end with the phrase "in Jesus' name." Rather he was emphasizing the importance of approaching God, not on the basis of our merits, but on the basis of what he has done for us. In other words, when, through faith, we are covered with Christ's righteousness, God is well-pleased with us and our prayers.

We need to remember that only believers' prayers please God, especially when one of our unbelieving friends is struggling with a problem. In such a situation, it is not good advice to tell them to pray about it! This only compounds their problem. It is much better to reassure them we will pray for them. We believers are the ones with access to God. We are the ones to whom God will listen.

Praying for others is what God tells us to do. "I urge, then, first of all, that petitions, prayers, intercession and thanksgiving be made for all people – for kings and all those in authority, that we may live peaceful and quiet lives in all godliness and holiness. This is good, and pleases God our Savior, who wants all people to be saved and to

[53] John 14:14 "You may ask me for anything in my name, and I will do it."

come to a knowledge of the truth" (1 Timothy 2:1-4). One of the best ways we can help people is by interceding for them. "The prayer of a righteous person is powerful and effective" (James 5:16).

The one thing prayer is not, however, is a source of revelation. In the previous chapters we have looked at some wonderful ways God communicates with us. He talks to us in his inspired word. He brings us the wonderful news of the gospel. He washes us in baptism and hugs us in his supper. Now, in prayer, he gives us the opportunity to talk to him: to sing his praises, to express our gratitude, to pour out our problems, to ask for his help.

At the risk of sounding like a broken record, I need to emphasize one more time how incredible this is. We don't have to make an appointment with God far in advance. We don't have to make sure we word our prayers exactly right. We don't have to limit ourselves to significant topics. Rather, as God's children, we can run into his throne room at any time and ask him anything. "The Spirit you received does not make you slaves, so that you live in fear again; rather, the Spirit you received brought about your adoption to sonship. And by him we cry, 'Abba, Father' (Romans 8:15).[54]

---

[54] Abba is a Hebrew word often used by small children to lovingly address their fathers.

As I mentioned above, prayer is a common activity of a believer. But may it never become commonplace. May we always cherish it as a wonderful gift from the ultimate humanitarian. "Now to him who is able to do immeasurably more than all we ask or imagine, according to his power that is at work within us, to him be glory in the church and in Christ Jesus throughout all generations, for ever and ever! Amen" (Ephesians 3:20-21).

For Further Reflection

1. Some people say James 1:5 teaches that the way to discern truth is by praying. "If any of you lacks wisdom, you should ask God, who gives generously to all without finding fault, and it will be given to you." This verse, however, isn't even talking about truth! It addresses a person who is lacking wisdom. Wisdom and truth are two completely different things. For example, the Bible says Jesus was "full of grace and truth" (John 1:14[55]). Jesus was truth personified. But it also says that, as a boy, he "grew in wisdom" (Luke 2:52[56]). Truth is objective, while wisdom is the subjective and wise application of truth. Some people might know the truth, but they aren't wise if they don't correctly act on the truth.

---

[55] John 1:14 The Word became flesh and made his dwelling among us. We have seen his glory, the glory of the one and only Son, who came from the Father, full of grace and truth.

[56] Luke 2:52 And Jesus grew in wisdom and stature, and in favor with God and man.

The context of James 1:5 shows the specific wisdom James is referring to: the correct understanding of and response to trials. The broader scriptural principle is that we can ask the Spirit for help whenever we are struggling in wisely applying a biblical teaching to a particular situation.

Truth, on the other hand, is discerned by comparing it to God's revealed truth in the Bible. "But even if we or an angel from heaven should preach a gospel other than the one we preached to you, let them be under God's curse! As we have already said, so now I say again: If anybody is preaching to you a gospel other than what you accepted, let them be under God's curse!" (Galatians 1:8-9).

2. Every Christian, at one time or another, has struggled with praying. Even in this situation, God comforts us wonderfully. "In the same way, the Spirit helps us in our weakness. We do not know what we ought to pray for, but the Spirit himself intercedes for us through wordless groans" (Romans 8:26). What a tremendous truth even though we can't fully understand it. God gives us this glimpse into his mysterious workings not to frustrate us, but to comfort us. This is how much God, the ultimate humanitarian, is personally involved in our lives!

Chapter Eighteen: A Humanitarian by Giving Us a Wonderful Life Here and Now

Occasionally someone suggests that the best scenario would be to come to faith late in life. They feel they will still go to heaven while they can enjoy life here! Such thinking reveals a tremendous lack of understanding on a number of levels. It exposes a weak view of sin's tyranny. Sometimes it demonstrates a warped view of the Christian life. (A man once told me he didn't want to become a Christian because he didn't want to give up bowling!) It almost always reveals considerable ignorance of the blessings *only believers* enjoy already here on earth.

Although God loves the entire world, he has a special love for believers. The Bible talks about the special relationship God has with believers. It records promises exclusively for believers. This special relationship and those tremendous promises translate into a wonderful life for believers right now.

Jesus said: "I have come that they may have life, and have it to the full" (John 10:10). Many people think Jesus is only referring to heavenly life. Heaven will definitely be incredible. It is also true, however, that the incredible life Jesus talks about begins as soon as a person believes.

When a person is brought to faith, *they immediately receive eternal life*. This surprises many people because they automatically associate eternal life with heaven. Listen, however, to what Jesus said: "Very truly I tell you, whoever hears my word and believes him who sent me has eternal life and will not be judged but has crossed over from death to life" (John 5:24). Jesus didn't say a believer will have eternal life. He *has* it as soon as he believes. Already he "*has crossed* over from death to life."

Obviously this doesn't mean believers are *fully* enjoying eternal life right now. The Bible uses the picture of God giving us the Holy Spirit as earnest money. "Now the one who has fashioned us for this very purpose is God, who has given us the Spirit as a deposit, guaranteeing what is to come" (2 Corinthians 5:5). What believers experience now is just a foretaste of what awaits them in heaven.

This, however, still translates into significant blessings already now. We have seen how totally engaged God was in saving us. From beginning to end, he did all the work. And he doesn't disengage once we are saved. It is thrilling to see how involved God remains in believers' lives.

Right now Jesus rules the universe with their welfare in mind. "God placed all things under his feet and appointed him to be head over everything *for the church*"

(Ephesians 1:22, my emphasis).[57] In a way which often remains hidden at the time, Jesus insures that world events will prosper believers. Sometimes he allows us to see this after the event. One good example is how the Lord used the persecution of the early Christians to spread the gospel. Other times his purposes remain hidden. Here too we must walk by faith and not by sight.

The sure knowledge that Jesus governs with believers' interests at heart gives tremendous peace in our turbulent world. Terrorists can threaten, leaders can stumble, markets can crash, hurricanes can hit, but through it all believers can remain calm and collected.

Jesus isn't just controlling world events either. He also works for believers on a personal level. "We know that in all things God works for the good of those who love him, who have been called according to his purpose" (Romans 8:28). Note this doesn't apply to everyone, but only "to those who love him," in other words, believers. No matter what happens to us personally, we can be confident the Lord will somehow work good from it.

There's more. Jesus not only *rules* for the believers' good. He also *intercedes* for them. "Christ Jesus who died

---

[57] In the Bible, the true church is the community of all believers and is not identified with any one visible organization. Sometimes people refer to it as the invisible church since only God can see who truly believes. "People look at the outward appearance, but the LORD looks at the heart" (1 Samuel 16:7).

– more than that, who was raised to life – is at the right hand of God and is also interceding for us" (Romans 8:34). He's not the only one interceding either. The Holy Spirit joins him. "In the same way, the Spirit helps us in our weakness. We do not know what we ought to pray for, but the Spirit himself intercedes for us through wordless groans" (Romans 8:26).

As holds true with so many actions of our awesome God, we can't comprehend what this intercession all entails. What comes through loudly and clearly, however, is that believers are not just numbers to God. On the contrary, "even the very hairs of your head are all numbered" (Matthew 10:30). This is how much the king of the universe loves us.

The bedrock of our faith is God working *for us.* Jesus fulfilled the law for us. He died for us. The Holy Spirit gave us faith. He, along with the Son, intercedes for us. Jesus now rules for us. As the ultimate humanitarian, God has worked and continues to work for us in diverse and wonderful ways.

But another important aspect of the eternal life believers enjoy is that Christ is *in us.* Paul proclaimed: "I have been crucified with Christ and I no longer live, but *Christ lives in me*" (Galatians 2:20, my emphasis). And

Christ is not alone either! 1 Corinthians 6:19[58] identifies believers as the temple of the Holy Spirit. Jesus also talks about he and the Father making their home with believers (John 14:23[59]).

This is another one of those biblical truths which boggle the mind. Even though we can't fully fathom it, we can treasure it. This is a very special relationship. The almighty, all majestic God lives within us! Saying this highly honors us sounds almost too trite.

Not only can we treasure this wonderful relationship, we can also make good use of it. The Lord's presence constitutes a great source of energy for believers. That is something Paul relied on. "To this end I strenuously contend with all the energy Christ so powerfully works in me" (Colossians 1:29). Tapping into Christ's power, believers can do great things. Jesus reassured his disciples: "I am the vine; you are the branches. If you remain in me *and I in you, you will bear much fruit;* apart from me you can do nothing" (John 15:5, my emphasis)

There's still more. Not only does the Lord give believers the *energy* to do good works, he also gives them

---

[58] 1 Corinthians 6:19 Do you not know that your bodies are temples of the Holy Spirit, who is in you, whom you have received from God? You are not your own;

[59] John 14:23 Jesus replied, "Anyone who loves me will obey my teaching. My Father will love them, and we will come to them and make our home with them."

opportunities for good works. "We are God's handiwork, created in Christ Jesus to do good works, *which God prepared in advance for us to do*" (Ephesians 2:10, my emphasis).

One of the greatest blessings a believer experiences is leading a God-pleasing, productive life. In spite of the danger of sounding like a broken record, I need to emphasize once again that this applies only to believers. As Jesus said, "apart from me you can do nothing" (John 15:5).

That only believers can do God-pleasing works already proves that good works *result* from salvation and do not *cause* it. Because they flow from faith the Bible refers to them as *fruit* (Matthew 3:8[60]). No place is the role of works seen clearer than in Ephesians 2:8-10. "For it is by grace you have been saved, through faith – and this is not from yourselves, it is the gift of God – *not by works*, so that no one can boast. For we are God's handiwork, created in Christ Jesus *to do good works*, which God prepared in advance for us to do" (my emphasis). We are not saved *by good works* – period. We are saved *to do good works* which glorify God and demonstrate our thankfulness to God. But as this passage emphasizes, those works contribute nothing to our salvation.

Many times when the topic turns to good works, believers hang their heads because they don't see

---

[60] Matthew 3:8 "Produce fruit in keeping with repentance."

themselves as having done them. That's natural as Jesus shows in his parable of the sheep and goats. When Jesus pointed out their good works, the believers didn't know what he was talking about. "Then the righteous will answer him, 'Lord, when did we see you hungry and feed you, or thirsty and give you something to drink? When did we see you a stranger and invite you in, or needing clothes and clothe you? When did we see you sick or in prison and go to visit you?'" (Matthew 25:37-39).

It is often difficult to see our good works because we still sin so much. Who of us can't relate with Paul? "For I do not do the good I want to do, but the evil I do not want to do – this I keep on doing" (Romans 7:19). Even though sin no longer *reigns* within us, it still *remains* in us – until the day we die.

The fact that we still sin doesn't mean we have to despair. Believers can be confident that their state of sinning doesn't affect their status as God's holy people! (See chapter 12). Shortly after bemoaning his inability to quit sinning, Paul exclaims: "There is now no condemnation for those who are in Christ Jesus" (Romans 8:1).

There's more. Not only is our status not affected by our sins, but our good works, even though they are tainted with sin, please God. So much so, that on Judgment Day we will hear God praising us. "Well done, good and faithful servant! You have been faithful with a few things;

I will put you in charge of many things. Come and share your master's happiness!" (Matthew 25:21).

I have cited only a few of the blessings God showers on believers. Everywhere we turn we see examples of his love. There are many others we don't even see. He is beyond generous in blessing believers. He is the ultimate humanitarian.

For Further Reflection

1. This chapter makes a sharp distinction between believers and unbelievers. One reason I emphasized the distinction is because it is frequently blurred. For example, sometimes Christians encourage their unbelieving friends by telling them God will work it out for their good. Or think of how people often comfort mourners by saying the deceased is in a better place, regardless of what the person believed. Or how the epitaph, "rest in peace" is applied indiscriminately. Blurring the difference between believers and unbelievers neither glorifies God nor helps people. What glorifies God and aids people is maintaining this distinction.

2. When sharing the gospel, believers often tell unbelievers they are just like them. It is their way to say they also sin. Over the years, however, I have found it helpful to highlight the difference between believers and unbelievers. Instead of saying I am like them, I now often say I used to be like them. I then proceed to tell them the wonderful things God has done for me and the great

things I now enjoy. Many people respond with curiosity to learn more.

3. A good exercise is to regularly reflect on the many blessings you have as a believer. Consider the peace of mind you enjoy – knowing you are at peace with God. Or the fact that angels serve you. "Are not all angels ministering spirits sent to serve those who will inherit salvation?" (Hebrews 1:14). Or that you can love sacrificially. "Dear friends, let us love one another, for love comes from God. Everyone who loves has been born of God and knows God" (1 John 4:7). The list goes on and on. As you read the Bible, keep a running record of verses which describe the blessings you enjoy right now as God's child.

Chapter Nineteen: A Humanitarian by Giving Us a Spectacular Eternity

Just as some don't fully value the wonderful life God has given believers already now, many don't appreciate the spectacular life they will enjoy in heaven. The cartoon of people sitting on clouds strumming harps is how more than a few picture it. They believe heaven will be boring. Sometimes believers even say they aren't ready to die because there are still things they want to enjoy on earth.

Paul didn't have that attitude. He said to die is *gain* (Philippians 1:21[61]). He knew death would instantly bring an end to all his problems. He understood heaven would be a most glorious, mind-boggling experience for him and all believers. But only for believers. Scripture clearly makes this distinction. "Whoever believes in the Son has eternal life, but whoever rejects the Son will not see life, for God's wrath remains on them" (John 3:36).

This glorious existence begins immediately when a believer dies. The Bible rules out the thought of an intermediate place where the souls of the departed go. A couple verses after saying his death would be gain, Paul talked about departing and *being with Christ.*

---

[61] Philippians 1:21 For to me, to live is Christ and to die is gain.

This applies to each and every believer. Through Jesus' merits, every single believer is worthy to dwell in God's presence for all eternity. Nowhere does the Bible talk about some in heaven not living with God. On the contrary, "God's dwelling place is now among the people, and he will dwell with them. They will be his people, and God himself will be with them and be their God" (Revelation 21:3).

By far, our greatest heavenly joy and glory will be living in God's presence. Think of how excited people become when they get the opportunity to meet someone they admire. Even if the meeting lasts only a few minutes, they view it as the experience of a lifetime. In heaven we will *remain* with God for all eternity. We will constantly be in his presence, experiencing unimaginable majesty and splendor. Not once will we be escorted out of his presence. For all eternity, we will experience his brilliant radiance.

And we will forever feel the warmth of his love. We have seen how God, in so many different and wonderful ways, has not only given tremendous gifts to humanity, but has also served them. Amazingly, his service doesn't come to an end in heaven! "The Lamb at the center of the throne will be their shepherd; 'he will lead them to springs of living water.' 'And God will wipe away every tear from their eyes'" (Revelation 7:17). Jesus the Lamb shepherding us. God wiping away our tears. A few chapters later that thought is repeated. "'He will wipe every tear from their eyes. There will be no more death' or mourning or crying or pain, for the old order of things has passed away" (Revelation 21:4). I can hardly wait!

This verse also illustrates that a good way to think about heaven is to talk about what won't be there. There will be no more death or even growing old. No more death also means there will be no more sin, because "the wages of sin is death" (Romans 6:23). This rules out even the possibility of our sinning. Imagine living with no temptation! That is truly unimaginable.

There will be no more crying or pain. No more physical pain – not even the slightest paper cut. No more weakness, weariness, or worries. "'Never again will they hunger; never again will they thirst. The sun will not beat down on them,' nor any scorching heat" (Revelation 7:16) We will not experience even the slightest discomfort.

No more pain includes more than physical pain. No longer will we experience the pain of unfinished tasks or missed opportunities. No more painful good-byes. No more hurt feelings or stepped-on toes. No more misunderstandings or wrong signals. Not even the slightest bit of friction in relationships. No more emotional pain. A totally pain-free life in all aspects. It is truly unimaginable.

Neither will we experience the pain of not having our unbelieving loved ones with us. I admit I don't know how this will be possible. Such pain, however, is included in God's banishment of all pain. Here is another place where we must walk in faith and take God at his word.

There is one other "no more" which sometimes troubles people: there is no marriage in heaven. "At the resurrection people will neither marry nor be given in marriage; they will be like the angels in heaven" (Matthew 22:30). Marriage is part of the old order of things which will pass away. Knowing how much our Lord loves us, we can be assured he has something much better in store for us.

This highlights one of the problems when talking about heaven. It's easier to think in terms of what won't be there. It's more difficult imagining the tremendous new things we will experience. Heaven, however, is not just about the absence of all negatives. It's mainly about new things – things we can't begin to imagine.

For example, in chapter 11 we touched on the glorified bodies God will give us. What does that exactly mean? Philippians 3:21[62] tells us our bodies will be like Jesus' resurrected body. The glimpses of the risen Lord the Bible affords us are tantalizing. He suddenly appears in a locked room. He suddenly disappears while eating with the two disciples from Emmaus. Obviously his body wasn't bound by time or place. What more is involved? We don't know. Jesus, however, says we will shine like the sun (Matthew 13:43[63]).

Or consider Psalm 16:11. "You make known to me the path of life; you will fill me with joy in your presence, with *eternal pleasures at your right hand*" (my emphasis). For all eternity, we will experience ever new delights. It will be like driving through a beautiful mountain range with a new and spectacular view around every curve. The last thing heaven will be is boring.

On another front, think of how exciting it will be to live with millions of angels. Or imagine the thrill of talking with Abraham, David, Paul, and all the other believers filling the pages of Scripture. Envision living with people from every period of history and from every nation. Think of the stories we will hear! Try to imagine the joy of getting

---

[62] Philippians 3:21 who, by the power that enables him to bring everything under his control, will transform our lowly bodies so that they will be like his glorious body.

[63] Matthew 13:43 "Then the righteous will shine like the sun in the kingdom of their Father. Whoever has ears, let them hear."

along perfectly with everybody. Picture yourself in the following:

> There before me was a great multitude that no one could count, from every nation, tribe, people and language, standing before the throne and before the Lamb. They were wearing white robes and were holding palm branches in their hands. And they cried out in a loud voice: "Salvation belongs to our God, who sits on the throne, and to the Lamb" (Revelation 7:9-10).

There is so much we don't know or can't comprehend about heaven. But God has given us these glimpses to excite us and create a yearning inside of us. Heaven is going to be an out of this world experience!

It's surprising, therefore, that believers don't think about it more frequently. If we knew we would be moving to an island paradise to live in a mansion, I think we all would think about it often, if not daily. We would try to find out as much as possible about it. We would day-dream about it. It's obvious from Paul's letters that is what he did in regard to heaven.

His focus on heaven helped him remain joyful and confident even when he suffered. As he told the Romans: "I consider that our present sufferings are not worth comparing with the glory that will be revealed in us" (Romans 8:18). This is saying a mouthful in light of how much Paul suffered.

Heaven is well worth keeping in sight. It is what everything in history has been building up to. It is what Jesus sacrificed to give us. It is the ultimate gift from the ultimate humanitarian.

For Further Reflection

1. The Bible frequently talks about our heavenly *inheritance*. "Praise be to the God and Father of our Lord Jesus Christ! In his great mercy he has given us new birth into a living hope through the resurrection of Jesus Christ from the dead, and into an inheritance that can never perish, spoil or fade. This inheritance is kept in heaven for you" (1 Peter 1:3-4).

Closely connected is the thought that we are *heirs*. "Now if we are children, then we are heirs – heirs of God and co-heirs with Christ, if indeed we share in his sufferings in order that we may also share in his glory" (Romans 8:17).

We don't know what this all entails. Again all we have are glimpses like the one in Revelation 3:21. "To the one who is victorious, I will give the right to sit with me on my throne, just as I was victorious and sat down with my Father on his throne." I don't know exactly what this means, but it does excite me all the more for heaven.

2. Often people talk about a loved one watching them from heaven. From a couple of perspectives, the Bible doesn't seem to support this. First, it is difficult to imagine how looking down on earth wouldn't give them some sadness and pain. And we know that both sadness and pain are banished in heaven.

Second, this doesn't seem to take into account the awe people will experience in heaven. They are in the presence of the majestic Lord. Imagine going on a trip away from home. You see incredible wonders and have stupendous experiences. You would be so caught up in them that you would not think of home. In heaven our awe is never-ending.

The bottom line is that there is nothing in the Bible to support such a thought and some things which speak against it. Finally, it is not important to have our departed loved ones watching us. What is important is knowing our gracious God is watching over us every moment. And this is something we definitely know.

Chapter Twenty: A Humanitarian by Giving Us a Perfect Revelation

God didn't just act wonderfully for the human race. He has also given us a record of his humanitarian efforts. This, in itself, demonstrates that he is a humanitarian. This is the record we have been exploring. This record, the Bible, is a wonderful gift itself.

The Bible is an amazing book. Persons who have dedicated their lives to studying it will be the first to admit they haven't mastered it. The more a person studies it, the more insights into our amazing God they will discover. The Bible is truly living and active (Hebrews 4:12[64]).

Shortly before he died, Paul wrote to Timothy: "From infancy you have known the Holy Scriptures, which are able to make you wise for salvation through faith in Christ Jesus. All Scripture is God-breathed and is useful for teaching, rebuking, correcting and training in righteousness, so that the servant of God may be thoroughly equipped for every good work" (2 Timothy 3:15-17). These words have the weight of someone who speaks from his deathbed. At such a time,

---

[64] Hebrew 4:12 For the word of God is alive and active. Sharper than any double-edged sword, it penetrates even to dividing soul and spirit, joints and marrow; it judges the thoughts and attitudes of the heart.

people only address the most important topics. It is significant that Paul felt it important to direct Timothy, his protégé, to the Scriptures.

He does this because they were breathed out by God. (Instead of "God-breathed," some translate "inspired.") The human writers were like sailboats propelled by the Holy Spirit. That is the picture Peter used in 2 Peter 1:20-21. "Above all, you must understand that no prophecy of Scripture came about by the prophet's own interpretation of things. For prophecy never had its origin in the human will, but prophets, though human, spoke from God as they were carried along by the Holy Spirit." In Greek the same word is used for both wind and spirit. In addition, the word translated "carried along" was often used in reference to ships. Thus the picture of a sailboat carried along when the wind fills its sails.

This doesn't describe just a general inspiration of thoughts. Every single word was breathed out by God. So much so that Paul bases an entire argument on the form of one Old Testament word! "The promises were spoken to Abraham and to his seed. Scripture does not say 'and to seeds,' meaning many people, but 'and to your seed,' meaning one person, who is Christ" (Galatians 3:16).

God breathed out the Old Testament in Hebrew and the New Testament in Greek. We don't possess any of the originals, only thousands of ancient copies. Although there are many different readings (variants) in these ancient copies, almost without exception, they are minor. Less than 1/10 of 1% are significant in the sense they change the meaning of a passage. Even in those cases, however, no biblical doctrine is affected. Regardless of what reading one follows, no new doctrine is introduced. This is truly remarkable. We can be assured that today's Hebrew and Greek Bibles are completely trustworthy.

This doesn't mean, however, that every translation is trustworthy. Some are good; others not so much. A sound practice is to refer to a number of translations in your Bible study.

Paul didn't just emphasize the Bible's *inspiration* to Timothy. He also stressed its *sufficiency*. First he said it was "able to make you wise for salvation through faith in Christ Jesus." We don't need any other scriptures or authorities teaching us about salvation. All we need is the Bible.

The same holds true for Christian living. The Bible is so useful, Paul said, that it thoroughly equipped the servant of God for every good work. It doesn't only partially equip people. It thoroughly equips them. Not just for some good works either, but "for every good work." The Bible tells us everything we need to know to please God. Not only that. It also empowers us to please God. We need nothing else. The Bible is totally sufficient.

Jesus emphasized the Bible's importance even after his resurrection. On Easter he appeared to two disciples as they walked to Emmaus. In the course of their conversation we read: "And beginning with Moses and all the Prophets, he explained to them what was said in all the Scriptures concerning himself" (Luke 24:27). Later that evening, he repeated the same thing to the rest of his disciples. "He said to them, 'This is what I told you while I was still with you: Everything must be fulfilled that is written about me in the Law of Moses, the Prophets and the Psalms.' Then he opened their minds so they could understand the Scriptures" (Luke 24:44-45). In this way, Jesus underscored Scripture's dominant place.

Jesus' threefold description of the Old Testament as "the Law of Moses, the Prophets and the Psalms" is also instructive. This was the normal way Jews described their Scriptures, the books we know as the Old Testament. By referring to them in this way, Jesus did not only give the Old Testament his stamp of authority, he also reassured us there were no lost scriptures. If any scripture would have been lost, we can be sure he would have made that known. *The Bible is inspired, sufficient, and complete.*

I would like to leave you with a few simple rules of biblical interpretation. One of the most essential is the principle of letting the Bible interpret the Bible. Since it is God's Word, it can't contradict itself. Thus an interpretation that contradicts a clear passage of Scripture can't be correct. Letting the Bible interpret itself also means that often a passage is made clear by another passage. One simple example is how John the Baptist's statement that Jesus was the Lamb of God (John 1:29[65]) helps us identify the Lamb mentioned in Revelation.

Although this principle is crucial, this is where much Bible interpretation falters. In order to use it, one naturally needs to know all the Bible. This takes work. But it is well worth it. Otherwise it is almost a certainty the interpretation will become skewed. In this regard, a cross-reference Bible is an excellent tool to aid you in letting the Bible interpret itself.

Another vital principle is reading passages in their context. I have as much of a chance of correctly understanding a verse pulled out of context as I do of understanding a movie by only viewing a two-minute scene from it. It is important to keep both the immediate and wider context in mind.

Finally, it is essential to always place God's revelation over our reason and emotion. Far too often people reject a biblical teaching because they can't understand it. Other times, they discard a teaching because of an emotional

---

[65] John 1:29 The next day John saw Jesus coming toward him and said, "Look, the Lamb of God, who takes away the sin of the world!"

response. (i.e. "I can't believe in a God who would send anybody to hell.") Let God's revelation reign supreme.

In this book I have attempted do just that. I have strived to get out of the way and let the beauty and power of God's Word dominate. It is my prayer that in some small way I have increased your appreciation for both our wonderful God and his wonderful word. It is my hope that you will be motivated to join me on this exhilarating journey of studying God's Word and continually learn more about God, the ultimate humanitarian.

"Praise be to the God and Father of our Lord Jesus Christ, who has blessed us in the heavenly realms with every spiritual blessing in Christ" (Ephesians 1:3).

For Further Reflection

"Consequently, you are no longer foreigners and strangers, but fellow citizens with God's people and also members of his household, built on the foundation of the apostles and prophets, with Christ Jesus himself as the chief cornerstone" (Ephesians 2:19-20). Throughout this book we have seen how Jesus is the church's cornerstone. Everything begins with him. Everything goes back to him. Everything receives direction from him. Now we want to consider how the apostles and prophets serve as the church's foundation.

Foundations are laid *in the beginning* of a building project. Although that is obvious, it bears pointing out. After foundations are laid, they aren't changed. That is why so much time is spent on blueprints. Altering the foundation after construction has begun is a recipe for failure.

The Lord is not a sloppy builder. He knew exactly on which foundation to build the church. And he laid the foundation *in the beginning* of the church's existence. He did it through the writings of the prophets and apostles: the Old and New Testaments. The Bible is the foundation on which the church is built.

This truth is seen in a number of different ways. One important fact is Paul's statement that he was the last apostle. In 1 Corinthians 15 he lists a number of appearances made by the risen Lord. He concludes by saying: "last of all he appeared to me also, as to one abnormally born" (v. 8). Paul compares himself to a child that a woman unexpectedly has late in life. No more apostles would come after him. He was the last one needed to lay the foundation.

The book of Hebrews supports this. It begins with the statement: "In the past God spoke to our ancestors through the prophets at many times and in various ways, but in these last days he has spoken to us by his Son" (Hebrews 1:1-2). "In the past" God spoke through prophets. But no longer. "In these last days" he spoke through the Son. He used the apostles to record his teachings.

Permit me to repeat: *the foundation of the apostles and prophets are the books of the Old and New Testament.* Everything is built on this foundation.

It is my prayer that you never stray from this foundation. Build your life on God's inspired word, especially those sections focusing on what God has done for you. Study them. Ponder them. Treasure them. Relax because of them. Be energized by them. Immerse yourself in God's Word: the word that describes our wonderful God – the ultimate humanitarian.

Acknowledgements

I would first like to acknowledge my family who plays such a big part in my life:

- My parents who are now both with the Lord. They didn't just teach me about our great God, they showed me what that meant each and every day as they lived trusting in him.

- Bonnie, my wonderful wife of over 40 years, who has served so faithfully behind the scenes. When our kids were small, you were the constant in their lives as I was serving as a busy pastor. Now, as I frequently travel for the ministry, you support me without complaint.

- Jenny, Erin, Adam, Jeremy, Tasha – our five kids. You are all wonderful mature Christians. We are so proud of each of you and pray that you remain strong.

- Jeremy, Ken, Tera, Stephanie, Adam – our five additional kids. We could not ask for better sons and daughters-in-law. Instead of bringing drama into our family, you have blended seamlessly into it.

➢ Our eleven grandkids. As you grow, may each of you grow strong in the Lord.

I would also like to acknowledge those who helped make this book a reality:

➢ Danee Haro and Christy Frey for going beyond the call of duty in doing all the detail work (editing, formatting, proof-reading) and getting the book ready for publication.

➢ Pastor Phil Koelpin for reviewing it especially from a theological perspective. Thank you for all your wise advice, valuable suggestions, and ongoing encouragement.

➢ Adam Dick for designing the book cover.

➢ John Sebald for your helpful advice in marketing and distribution.

➢ Phil Koelpin, Dan Kunz, Robert Timmerman, Denny Walters, Tom Walters, Bill Woodington – not only for your service on the board of Truth in Love Ministry, but especially for your passion for the ministry and for your unfailing support and encouragement. You are not only good board members but great friends!

- The members of the focus groups who gave me many suggestions and much encouragement through the writing process.

- The many friends of our ministry who gave me so much support and words of encouragement.

About the Author

Mark J. Cares has been a pastor for over thirty years, graduating from Wisconsin Lutheran Seminary in 1977. He planted a congregation in Boulder, Colorado and then served a congregation in Idaho for many years. During that time, he extensively studied Mormonism and developed a loving approach to sharing Christ with them. This approach is explained in detail in his book, *Speaking the Truth in Love to Mormons*.

He presently serves as the founder and president of Truth in Love Ministry, a ministry dedicated to training Christians to witness to Mormons. Contact us at tilm@tilm.org or visit tilm.org to learn more.